W9-CNG-114

a
crash course
on

Financial
Statements

a crash course on

on

Financial Statements

By David Bangs

EP
Entrepreneur.
Press

Publisher: Jere L. Calmes
Cover Design: Andrew Welyczko
Production and Composition: CWL Publishing Enterprises, Inc., Madison, WI

This publication is designed to provide accurate and authoritative information
in regard to the subject matter covered. It is sold with the understanding that
the publisher is not engaged in rendering legal, accounting or other professional
services. If legal advice or other expert assistance is required, the services of a
competent professional person should be sought.

Library of Congress Cataloging-in-Publication Data

Bangs, David H.
  A Crash course on financial statements / by David Bangs.
    p. cm.
  Includes bibliographical references.
  ISBN-13: 978-1-59918-384-8 (alk. paper)
  ISBN-10: 1-59918-384-6
  1. Small business--Finance. 2. Business enterprises--Finance. 3. Financial
statements. I. Title.

  HG4027.7.B3477 2010
  658.15'1--dc22

                                                        2010010242

14 13 12 11 10   10 9 8 7 6 5 4 3 2 1

Contents

To the Reader

The primary aim of *A Crash Course On Financial Statements* is to help you take advantage of the information contained in your financial statements. That information, some of it highly compressed and not apparent at first reading, will help you control your business. Without that information you'll be flying blind. With it, you can manage your business to generate profits, build value, and secure the right financing for growth. Remember: financial control is the key to profitability.

Small businesses often have difficulty obtaining outside financing, whether from individual investors, banks, finance companies or institutional investors. The Small Business Administration (SBA) was established to help small businesses get the financing they need, but given the current problems in the banking industry, they can't do much. When major banks cut down their lending, small businesses are the first to feel the crunch.

These tough economic conditions won't go away quickly. As a

small business owner, what can you do to get the credit and/or capital investment you need?

Plenty. The key to obtaining financing is the same as ever: Be prepared. There are lenders and investors out there. They want to put money into sound businesses—that is, businesses that can provide them with a decent return on their investment, realistic risks and rewards, and timelines for return of their capital. In the country as a whole, credit unions, local and small regional banks, and investors serving local markets are more willing to lend to small businesses than the giant national and international banks.

What does "be prepared" mean? For *A Crash Course On Financial Statements*, it means doing your homework. You have to consider economic conditions, make sure you are creditworthy, know how much financing you need, and when you need it. You have to make sure that you're fully invested in your business—and above all you have to be prepared to show why an investment in your small business is a good idea.

There's a logical flow to obtaining financing. **Part One: Be Prepared to Be Prepared** starts with an overview of the information you need, both financial and non-financial. Bankers and equity investors want to invest in well-run, profitable businesses, which means that you have to keep your business under tight financial control. This is the *controlling* part. **Part Two: The Financial Statements** is a review of the basic financial statements all businesses need to use. **Part Three: Reading and Analyzing Financial Statements** puts the financials to use in controlling your business. Ratios and comparisons are the main tools but there are others perhaps less familiar to you. **Part Four: Using the Financials to Manage Your Business** introduces more techniques to use the financials to manage and improve your business. **Parts Five** and **Six** look toward securing financing for your business. Banks receive the most attention, since that's where small businesses traditionally get their financing. Other sources, some outlandish, are also considered.

Managing and controlling the finances of your business are the keys to getting the financing you need. It really is that simple. The money is out there, the will to lend and invest is still strong, and the economy will eventually turn around.

The last two sections draw heavily on *Financing a Small Business*, a most helpful book published by Entrepreneur Press a few years back. I often argue against reinventing the wheel—what has been done well can, with permission of the publisher, be updated and continue to do a good service.

Finally, a big thank you to Jere Calmes, an old crony and the reason this book was written. It's good to get back into the writing game, especially when the industry is in contraction. Jere and I have worked together for many years, always amicably. May I dedicate this book to you, Jere?

Andy Bangs
Portsmouth, NH

a
crash course
on

Financial
Statements

Part One

Be Prepared to Be Prepared

Before Seeking Financing

Organize Your Information Needs

Decisions come in three modes: hunch-based, habit-based, and information-based. The last of these is best, since it can include the first two while testing them on an ongoing basis. Hunches are fine. They provide insights into your business, encourage you to enter new markets in spite of apparent obstacles, and generate energy and excitement. However, for every successful hunch there are several failed hunches. The hunch tested against information gains you the best of both worlds. Your hunch is a reflection of your experience and intelligence, and the information is a backup.

Habits are also useful. They save time and free you to do more than you could otherwise do. But if you don't occasionally step back and check to make sure that your habits are indeed useful, you may find yourself in counterproductive ruts.

Rather than risk disaster (assuming these are major decisions), make sure that you have a reasonable information base to test your hunches and habits before charging ahead. Over time your decisions will only be as good as the information on which you base them.

Ensuring a clear, consistent, coherent, and timely information flow is no easy task. You need your accountant's skills to make sure you get the right financial information (more on this in Chapter 2). You might want to call a consultant to set up your information system—you know what information would be desirable to have in many instances, and what timing is needed.

Your information needs will vary. As a general rule, cost of information, timeliness, level of detail, and applicability are the most important considerations. Your time is valuable. So you need organized, concise information that sums up the activities of your company in a useful way.

 KEY INFO

▶ Six Steps to Organizing Information Needs

The six steps of organizing your information needs will help you get what you need, when you need it, at a price and level of detail that makes sense for your company.

1. Outline and prioritize the ten most important decisions you have to make.
2. List the business activities you want to monitor.
3. Collect data.
4. Organize the data in standard forms.
5. Use the data. Schedule time to review the information.
6. Implement information flow. Review it periodically.

Outline Your Ten Most Important Decisions

The first step in establishing the right information flow for your business is to take a close look at the important decisions you have to make in the near future. As a practical exercise this has several benefits.

First, it is an excellent planning tool. You have a number of decisions you're expected to make, some of which are more important than others. Yet if you're like most people, you seldom take time to prioritize decisions in terms of potential impact, importance, and long-term effects.

Second, as you list the ten most important decisions you face, you'll probably find that the first five or six are obvious. The reminder takes a bit more thought. Why ten? You want to make sure that you cover the ground thoroughly. The first few times you try this exercise you'll probably come up with longer or different lists. Write them all down. Review them and try to generate what are *prima facie* the most important ten.

TABLE

#	Decision to Be Made:	Information Needed
1		
2		
3		
4		
5		
6		
7		
8		
9		
10		

#	Aardvark's Decisions to Be Made:	Information Needed
1	How best to deal with COGS? It's 65%; want to lower it to 60% by 12/11.	
2	Is our product mix optimal?	
3	Brad's leaving. Do we need a new salesperson?	
4	Old plant is falling apart. Best way forward?	
5	Delivery service needs to be put out to bid.	
6	Spiff up the store? Or enjoy its charm?	
7	Continuing problem with slippage.	
8	Trade shows – are they paying off?	
9	Nephew needs a job... can we use him?	

Check over your completed list. Ask yourself the following questions:

▶ Can I make a decision based on the information I have available? Would more information help?
▶ Ideally, what information would I use to make the decision?
▶ Can I get that information? How? When? At what cost?
▶ What is the minimum amount of information I would feel comfortable with?

Rank the decisions in terms of long-range impact. This will help you focus on the more important problems. It may be useful to remember that it doesn't matter how hard you row, but it does matter that you are in the right boat.

Ask yourself: What important decision(s) have I been putting off? Why?

Most of us know that there are decisions that for one reason or another we're avoiding. These can include financial decisions (Can we afford to expand?), strategic decisions (Should we enter that market?), and/or emotionally painful decisions (Should I fire Harry?). In all major decisions, well-organized information will make a positive difference. As an example: You'd better not fire Harry unless you can document the reasons for firing him: days absent without excuse, actions that received warnings, data about giving him warnings, and signed affirmations that he understood the warnings.

The purpose of the list (and of the questions the list raises) is to find a starting point for establishing the right information flow for your business, based on your knowledge of its operations and goals. Refining the list can come later. For now, the list alone will be useful.

List Activities to Monitor

Which activities should you monitor? Some of the obvious ones are cash flow, sales levels, credit, and collection actions. Your financial statements provide information about most of the business activities, but there are many other important activities to monitor. How about employee performance (both individual and by department)? What have been the results of marketing and advertising efforts?

Collect Accurate Data

Raw data is generated by any attempt to record what goes on in a business. Usually, activities are measured in terms of money, units, or time. Cash flow is measured in dollars and time. How does cash in motion operate? To keep tabs on sales personnel, you need call reports and sales information. Where are purchases being made for inventory, administrative use, and so on?

This step almost always requires professional advice. The generation and ordering of raw data is where your accountant earns praise or blame. Hiring a first-rate accountant is a good investment.

Organize the Data

Raw data has to be shaped before you can use it. Summarize the information as it's generated. For most businesses, this requires standard financial statements: balance sheet, income statements, statements of cash flow. These are compilations of the myriad transactions that a business performs. Otherwise, you'd get buried in a flood of raw data.

Don't put the financials aside "until we have time for them." The financials are supposed to help you manage your business more profitably. Set a specific time to go over your financials at least once a month, preferably more often.

Learning too late about a problem or opportunity is no way to run a business. One of the measures of managerial performance is to see how quickly you can identify and capitalize on new opportunities— and how quickly you can solve problems.

For sales and marketing control, you need a way to summarize salespeople's performance on a weekly or monthly basis. Ask for a summary of calls made, orders placed, customer suggestions, criticisms, and other ideas.

For personnel decisions, some basic information is (legally) mandatory. To evaluate people fairly, document what they do. What about attendance? What about performance against mutually agreed-on goals? The potential list is endless.

Use the Data

The next step is to interpret the data and put it to work. A cash flow report isn't informative in and of itself. It has to be compared to some standard—that is, interpreted—before it becomes useful. Often the standard is historical: What is the trend? Is the cash flow positive or negative, and how does that compare to the last several periods? How does profitability compare to trade averages, past performance, budget?

That's your job. Data gathering and compilation is just the starting point. You can't delegate the interpretation and application if you're the boss.

The financial statements contain a huge amount of information (hence the need for books such as this). As the owner/manager your time is limited. Get to know the financials well. They are the key to financing and controlling your business. Look for deviations, changes, and departures from the norm. These are where you'll find problems

KEY INFO

▶ Use the Data

1. Measure activities selectively.
2. Compile information into reports (summaries, compilations).
3. Make sure these are timely and useful to you, not just to the experts.
4. Compare summaries with standards (goals) and take action where needed.

or opportunities. How often you do this depends; if cash flow is a problem, weekly or even daily attention may be called for. If sales are slow, look at daily sales reports. If there's a problem with receivables, check them weekly.

But remember: If you don't have standards by which to measure cash flows, sales, or collections, all the data in the world won't help you.

Implement Information Flow

Make your information flow a managerial priority to be reviewed at least once a year. If there's a major change in your business, review and adjust the system. You set the standards using your knowledge and experience. Make sure that you can recognize when exceptions occur.

How much time does it take to implement an appropriate information flow strategy? Less than you might think, since a large part of it can be performed by outside advisors. You may not want to hire a consultant (except the accountant and lawyer), so consider the following sources of help:

▶ **Trade journals and trade shows**
▶ **Your banker**
▶ **SBA resources, especially the Small Business Development Centers and SCORE (Service Corps of Retired Executives) programs**
▶ **Chamber of Commerce**

There's no need to reinvent the wheel. Trade shows are a great place to compare notes with other people in your line of business. The

SBA (sba.gov) is a vast repository of helpful information and forms.

Information is power. Repeat: Information is power. The more information you can put to work, the better your business will be.

▶ Managing By Information

The overall performance of your business is built from the innumerable daily activities performed by you and your employees. Financial statements and daily journals cover some of these activities, but not all, and not even all of the important activities.

The idea behind managing by information—by the numbers—is that you can control what you can measure, and what gets measured gets done.

If you can measure performance, you can manage and improve the results. Your employees want and need to know what they're required to do. Objective measures, agreed to by you and your employees beforehand, are a way to convey such knowledge. More important, knowing what they're required to do helps improve their performance. Most people like to know whether they are doing a good job and seek feedback so they can improve their performance. Other employees, the ones you'd rather not have, can be encouraged to change or sometimes frightened away by the imposition of clear, objective, measurable performance standards. In the unhappy event that you have to fire someone, a paper trail documenting failure to meet agreed-on minimum performance standards goes a long way toward defusing potential legal claims.

Deciding what to measure and how to measure it isn't always easy. Fortunately, help is available. Just about every aspect of human behavior has been studied, measured, analyzed, and argued over by generations of intelligent people. Business is no exception. Within your trade association you can find more ways to measure what you do than you'll ever use.

What about sales? You can measure the number of prospecting calls and letters, number of cold calls per week, number of presentations or proposals made, number of contacts needed to close a sale, and number and profitability of sales. All help pin-point where a sales problem is rooted.

It does require work. Finding the key measures for individu-als and processes takes savvy and research. Keeping track takes constant effort. Some employees will resist (try getting sales-people to file call reports if they aren't used to them) keeping accurate records, and a few may falsify records. But over the long haul, managing by information pays off in dollars, self-esteem, and job satisfaction.

2

Get a Certified Public Accountant to Set Up Your Books

B asic business activities are the same for all businesses: buying and selling. There are no exceptions. You have to keep track of sales and expenses. You have to keep track of what you own and what you owe. You have to maintain sufficient records to keep the IRS from getting cross. Depending on the state, county, and city your business is located in, you will have sales, income, and other taxes to pay.

The more of this basic information you can gather the better. It will allow your accountant to get right to work on your behalf, rather than spending his or her time scouting up industry-specific formats and information that you could have found in your spare time.

Why Hire An Accountant?

If you don't know why you need an accountant, you're too naive to be in business. If you can't afford to pay for an accountant, you're under-capitalized and won't survive long.

Why hire an accountant? For the financial management and tax expertise they bring to your business. Accountants are trained to set up your books, gather data, and reshape it into highly formatted financial statements, and then draw judgments from the information. A good accountant will help you deal with bankers and other investors and suggest the right kinds of controls and economies. They know a lot about how to finance a business and smooth out cash flows.

Good accountants quickly develop sensitivity to the needs of the small businesses they work with. They can and will draw attention to drawbacks in your financial plans. This holdback function is extremely important for most entrepreneurs, who are blinded by enthusiasm to the pitfalls in their plans. This role of devil's advocate is invaluable.

Taxes are the least important reason to hire a capable accountant. The role of the accountant is to help you get the information you need, when you need it, in a form that enables you to make better decisions. This doesn't mean your accountant's role in minimizing your tax liabilities is unimportant. Your main job is to make a profit so you have to pay taxes, and you should run your business accordingly. Tax considerations affect profitability (there is no such thing as a pre-tax profit), but are secondary to the main purpose.

Some business owners hire one accountant for tax purposes and another for managerial reasons. Although this is extreme and too expensive for most small businesses, the skills required in tax work are not the same as those required in helping you run your business more efficiently. A common complaint about accountants is that they look backward, not toward future events, and are in some instances little more than expensive bookkeepers. You wouldn't turn to your accountant for advice on an aggressive growth strategy, though you should ask his or her advice on whether you can afford that growth, and if not, what your options might be.

Do not reinvent the information system. Do your research, ask questions, keep notes, and let your accountant set up your books and recommend the most appropriate accounting method for your business.

What Information Do You Need?

Most small businesses can be run with monthly statements (balance sheet, cash flow pro forma, and profit & loss). Some businesses need information more often. Some retailers want daily sales and customer count information, which they use to compare with previous years on a day-to-day basis.

Just learning what information you can use is a major undertaking. If you're experienced in your line of business, you may or may not know what information you need. Do what a beginner would do: ask. Start with trade sources, including the trade association magazines and newsletters, editors and consultants to the trade, and other experts. The costs will be trivial compared to the savings in accountant charges. The most successful businesses in your line are the ones who know what information they need and when they need it. Emulate them—at least until you have better ideas.

Details differ from business to business, but the financial structure of businesses in the same line as you is the best starting point. One way to look at this is that the financial skeletons are similar, but the flesh that goes on those bones will vary dramatically, depending on the age and stage of the business.

Get copies of other business' Chart of Accounts. The Chart of Accounts forms the backbone of your general ledger, which is the core of your accounting system. Whether you use a simple pegboard system or a sophisticated computerized system, you need a Chart of Accounts. Your accountant will have ideas of what he would like you to have, not necessarily tailored to your information needs. If you tell him what you want to keep track of, and why, and what you may want to track in the future, your books can be set up to make the information available.

Selecting An Accountant

Unless you've been trained as an accountant and have considerable experience, to decide what to track and what to ignore is too important to try to do yourself. The false economy of doing it yourself is highly dangerous. While doing it yourself may appear to be a way to save much-needed cash, it isn't. You won't get the kind of information you need, you won't get accurate information, and what you do get won't be timely enough to make your managerial tasks easier.

There are some short cuts you can take to keep your accounting bills to a sensible minimum. The more precise your questions to your accountant can be, the lower the bill.

Step 1: Know Your Needs and Goals Before You Seek an Accountant

Start by seeking trade information. What do businesses in your field keep track of? How do they keep on top of their information needs? If you can, get sample financial statements from businesses like yours. Your trade association can provide samples and will be able to steer you to sources of specific financial information ranging from seminars and study groups to consultants specializing in your kind of business.

Step 2: Consult with Friends, Colleagues, and Business Associates

Talk with other business owners. Ask them whom they recommend, what problems they have with their accountants, and what questions to ask when interviewing accountants.

Talk with your bankers. Most bankers keep a list of accountants they feel comfortable recommending to small business owners.

Check with your vendors. They tend to know who the good professionals are in your area.

Use local business groups such as the chamber of commerce as a preliminary screen.

KEY INFO

▶ Questions to Ask

Questions to ask your banker, friends, colleagues, and business associates:

- ▶ Whom do you recommend?
- ▶ Are you happy with the information you now get?
- ▶ How would you improve your information systems?
- ▶ How often do you use your financials: weekly, monthly, or quarterly? (Waiting for year-end is foolish. You need financial information at least monthly.)
- ▶ What does your accountant help you with?
- ▶ Does he or she help with pricing decisions?
- ▶ What are the key financial items you follow? Gross sales, gross margins, operating expenses, cash balance?
- ▶ What non-financial information do you keep track of?

(For example: number of items kept in stock, unit shipments, number of sales calls made, daily customer counts. This kind of information can be very valuable, especially if you are relatively new to the business.)

▶ If you could only have three pieces of information, what would they be? (Many business owners insist on keeping ongoing track of sales revenue, gross margin, and profit or loss. Manufacturers track billings, bookings, and backlog.)

▶ Are you happy with your accounting software? What do you use?

Step 3: Compare Advantages and Disadvantages of Large or Small Accounting Firms

Accountants come in various degrees. Certified Public Accountants (CPAs) are the most professional with credentials based on education and experience. They are expensive and may not be necessary for your business. Many small businesses get along just fine with public accountants or with "business counselors" affiliated with franchises such as General Business Service. While these accountants and advisors are not as credentialed as CPAs, they may be just as expert in small business matters, or more so—some CPA firms are uneasy in dealing with small businesses, and major CPA firms (regional or national) won't put their most experienced hands to work on your problems. Instead, you'll get the newest kid on the block.

Public accountants and business counselors are apt to specialize in small businesses and make their living from helping these businesses grow and prosper. Small business owners tend to remain with local firms. By concentrating on small business, they learn the quirks and whims of running small, undercapitalized companies, acquire a depth of small business financial knowledge that is deeper and more detailed than a Big Six accounting firm junior accountant, and become founts of knowledge about local conditions. The tradeoffs (there are always tradeoffs, unfortunately) are that these accountants and counselors aren't as well-versed in tax minutia, don't have the big banking and financial connections of CPAs, and may be less sophisticated than you might wish.

The most common reason to hire a CPA—whether independent or a member of an accounting firm—is that only CPAs can audit your books. This can be important for bankers and other investors. On the other hand, most small businesses don't have to provide audited statements, and the substantial added expense of audited statements could be avoided. However, the comfort factor that CPAs afford bankers, even if they give a qualified opinion rather than an audit, may be worth the added cost.

Step 4:   Set Up Personal Interviews with Several Accountants

Once you have a list of three or more accountants who seem to meet your needs, call on them. Make appointments, tell them what you're looking for, and what you think you might need to spend.

When you interview accountants, remember that they're in business too. Just as you wouldn't hire a doctor purely on cost comparisons, don't hire an accountant just because she's the cheapest in town. Sometimes that's an expensive way to go. Some of the questions to ask your prospective accountants include:

1. Have you worked with businesses like mine before? If not, are you willing to learn about my kind of business?
2. Can you put me in touch with some of your clients and some of your former clients?
3. What are your charges?
4. Do you charge a retainer or do you bill only for work performed?
5. If you don't think you'd be the right accountant/firm for me, could you recommend some accountants who might be right?

Step 5:   Ask for References; Check Them

Make sure to get a list of clients, both current and former, so you can find out what working with the accountant has been like for others. Former clients may be more revealing than current clients, and of course the accountant wants to present his or her most contented clients.

When you check with the references, ask:

1. How responsive are they (the accounting firm)?
2. Do you get reports and filings on time?
3. How well do they work with you?

4. Can they help with banking relationships?

5. Do you feel you can level with them?

6. Would you recommend that I hire them?

Everybody (or almost everybody) likes to be helpful. You'll find the references eager to talk about their experiences. Don't waste time asking for references and not following up with them.

Step 6: Get an Engagement Letter

Ask the accountant you choose to provide you with an engagement letter. This spells out the details of the arrangement between your company and the accountant. An engagement letter will cover:

1. **The professional undertaking** (set up books, provide monthly compilations, provide tax advice, and so on)
2. **Hourly fees**
3. **Other fee arrangements** (retainers, contingency fees)
4. **Costs** (expenses they bill you for, such as travel, office expenses, etc.)
5. **Late payments**
6. **File retention and destruction**
7. **Termination by either party**
8. **Special arrangements**

There may be other items in the engagement letter, but the underlying purpose is clear. Hiring an accountant (accounting firm, CPA, PA, or business counselor) is a serious matter. Both sides have to know what's expected of the other. It's important to have a prior agreement to deal with the inevitable hassles that arise when two parties work closely together.

KEY INFO

▶ Common Sense Precautions

The mechanics of bookkeeping and record keeping are important. You need consistency and accuracy, which in turn demands that the mechanics be simple and direct. Complicated systems don't work; they get in the way. To assure a clean flow of information, some common sense precautions apply.

▶ **Keep written records.** Nobody has a memory keen enough to track all the transactions a business undergoes.

▶ **Use a checkbook for all disbursements.** "Petty cash" accounts tend to be overused in small businesses and lead to unnecessary waste, as well as a woeful lack of information. Money dribbles away. The discipline of writing a check mysteriously cuts costs. It also provides a fine record of what was spent, when.

▶ **Use technology.** Electronic cash registers and scanners are worth the investment, since they provide a track of receipts and help you manage inventory. If you find that businesses like yours usually use computers, scanners, or other technologies, take it as a hint. Use sales books, including duplicate sales receipts.

The time these tools save pays off the investment in them fast. They are inexpensive insurance against pilferage and fraud. Clear, updated records have a deterrent effect on the light-fingered.

▶ Finding a New Accountant

You have to get along with your accountant. You need a financial advisor you can level with and whose opinions you can trust. If you want some point more fully explained or are worried about the business, an accountant can be a good friend to have. If you are putting together a financing proposal, you need someone who can tell you whether the numbers hang together. As with any professional, you need one who will give you the unvarnished truth.

How do you go about finding the right accountant for your business? If you already have an accountant and aren't sure you're getting the service you deserve, act as if you were new in town. You aren't obligated to stay with an accountant if you don't want to. You want to find a number of apparently qualified accountants (CPAs, Pas, or business counselors), and then choose from this pool of qualified professionals.

3

▼

Key Steps to Obtain Financing

When should you start to think about securing financing for your venture? All of the time. Not just when a cash crunch threatens your business, or payroll can't be met—that's too late. One often overlooked key to obtaining financing is to manage your business in such a way that you can meet any realistic criteria for obtaining financing. This is sometimes called "being bankable." As you become familiar with financial statements and their use in controlling your business, some more technical ways of analyzing and presenting your finances will emerge. (These will be treated in **Part Five: Using the Financials to Finance Your Business: How to Secure the Right Bank Financing at the Right Time for *Your* Business.**)

Preparation is the key to getting the right financing. You can't go to your family, your banker, or any other potential investor, ask for money for your business without a sensible rationale for both the amount and the purpose, and expect to receive a favorable response. And now that credit is tight and investors are wary, you have to make an even better case than in normal times.

So what can you do? There are eight basic steps to follow:

1. **Look at economic conditions.** It's harder to get financing when the economic outlook is cloudy, or when the local economy is in a tailspin.
2. **Make sure you're qualified.** Some obvious disqualifiers include poor credit history, lack of or insufficient profits, too much debt, defection of key employees, industry-wide contraction, too much competition, and lack of a viable niche in the market. Some of these can be changed. You may be better off to postpone seeking financing until conditions improve.
3. **List the apparent reasons you need financing.** The three big areas are working capital, purchasing assets, and funding growth.
4. **Check for unused or underused resources, both personal and in the business.** Your personal assets have to be deeply invested in your business before you can obtain financing. Make sure your budgets (personal and business) are lean.
5. **Calculate the amount of money you need.** You may need money for more than one reason. Talk with your banker. You may be able to stage funding—so much now, so much when you reach a certain goal. Changes in current assets and liabilities provide a clue to how much you need to raise. So does the cash flow pro forma.
6. **Determine what kind of financing is appropriate for your business at this time.** Debt, equity, or other? You may be able to refinance, work out a better lease, or sell off an asset.
7. **Decide when the money is needed.** Your cash flow pro forma helps you determine the timing pressures you will face. If your plans include expansion or acquisition of a competitor, what's the optimal timing?
8. **Explain why this financing package is a wise investment for your prospective investors (including yourself).** This may be the most important step of all. Your financing proposal has to make the case that this is a prudent investment, that it makes the business stronger and more profitable, and that there is a very low risk of capital loss.

4

What Do Bankers Want?

Banks provide 65 percent of business financing—a good reason to understand how bankers think.

The main concern bankers have is to protect their capital, money that their depositors have entrusted them with. Consequently, bankers are very conservative. Their first priority is to recoup the principal of the loan. Their next priority is to earn a reasonable rate of interest on the loan. And their third priority is that you prosper and open more accounts with them. Safety of principal is paramount. Bankers are not in the risk business.

Your job is to provide the banker with as many reasons to feel safe as you can. You start with a loan or financing proposal. A *loan proposal* is a documented statement of what debt you need, why you need it, when you need it, and how you plan to repay it. The documentation should include a description of how much you need and what you'll do with the loan, up-to-date balance sheets, cash flow pro formas, and projected income statements. All banks have forms to help you prepare these but by using your own business plan, you increase your credibility (see Chapters 19 and 24.).

What do bankers look for when considering a financing proposal? The "Six Cs of Credit" provides a start.

KEY INFO

▶ **The Six Cs of Credit**

1. **Character:** Personal character is most important, since all loans to small businesses are personal loans. The bank's experience with you is critical. The judgment on the character of an individual is based on past performance. Personal credit histories as well as business credit histories will be reviewed.

2. **Capacity:** This is figured on the amount of debt load that your business can support. The debt-to-net worth (debt/net worth) ratio is often used to justify a credit decision. A highly leveraged business with a high debt/net worth is perceived as less creditworthy than a company with low leverage (low debt/net worth). Your business plan can make a difference. Suppose it shows that the loan will increase earnings and lead to a swift reduction in the debt/net worth ratio. Your chances of a positive answer would increase. Keep in mind that a good banker—and you can't afford an inept banker who loads you up with unnecessary debt—is the ultimate realist. Don't try to snow your banker with numbers.

3. **Conditions:** Economic conditions, both regional and national, have a profound effect on credit decisions. If the bank is persuaded that a depression is coming, it won't extend credit easily.

4. **Collateral:** Collateral is a secondary source of loan repayment. They want the loan repaid from operating profits and inventory turn so you become a bigger, better borrower and depositor. But just in case things go sour, a bit of collateral makes your banker sleep better at night.

5. **Credibility:** Do you know your business? Can you be counted on to be level-headed? How credible are your

plans? Are they a collage of dreams or a carefully reasoned and researched plan with a high chance of success? A business plan helps you answer the banker's questions without hesitation, sending your credibility rating soaring.

6. **Contingency Plan:** A contingency plan is a useful financing tool. Bankers like to see that you look ahead. A contingency plan proves forethought. A contingency plan is a short worst-case business plan that examines the options that would be open to the business and how those options would be treated. Decisions made in panic are poor decisions. A contingency plan avoids panic (both yours and your banker's).

Keep in mind that all small business loans are personal loans. Personal guarantees support the great majority of small business credits. Some magazine article writers and other "experts" argue that you shouldn't personally guarantee loans to your business, but apparently they have never been in business or been bankers. Refuse to guarantee the loan, and prepare to turn elsewhere for financing (which you won't get). Bankers, being realists, know that if you don't have a personal stake in the credit, it's easy to walk away from it. So they will ask you to sign on all notes both as an officer or owner of the business and as an individual. The pundits who say you shouldn't personally guarantee your business's loans enjoy fantastical notions about the impermeability of the corporate shield. In the real world, incorporation of a small business affords no protection whatsoever to the owners. If the business goes broke, the creditors will successfully go after the assets of the owners. So don't worry about signing loan guarantees. If you are squeamish about signing them, it's a clear signal to your banker that you don't believe in your business, your plans, or yourself. Why would you expect the banker to have more faith in your abilities than you do?

Why do bankers turn down loan applications? Except for bank credit policy reasons or banking law, applications are rejected for the following credit-related reasons:

▶ **Too little owner's equity**
▶ **Poor earnings record**

▶ **Questionable management**
▶ **Low-quality collateral**
▶ **Slow/past due trade or loan payment record**
▶ **Inadequate accounting system**
▶ **Startup or new company**
▶ **Poor moral risk**
▶ **Other** (only 4 percent of rejections have other reasons)

Take your banker to lunch. Always be honest with him or her. It pays. Make appointments before dropping in. Bankers are business people, and appreciate ordinary business courtesy. Keep in mind that your relationship with your banker should be cooperative, not antagonistic, subservient, fawning, obsequious, mistrustful, or fearful. A good banker is a terrific asset, so shop around to find a banker you can work with. The role of your banker is to help you make your business successful. A good banker will sometimes do things that you don't agree with such as turn down a loan request, or try to get you to maintain a cautious debt/net worth ratio. How do you find a good banker? Ask around. Ask other business owners, ask your accountant or lawyer, or other advisors. Ask your friends. Think of it as shopping for a partner: what would you do to find a person who can help make your business more successful?

Know the kind of credit you need. The basic rule is to fit the term of the loan to the purpose. A real estate loan will run fifteen years or more, and be repaid from operating profits, while an inventory loan is short-term, and gets repaid from the inventory turn. Some loans call for term payments that include principal and interest, others for interest only with lump sum principal reductions. The package can become complex. If in doubt, ask your bankers for advice: "I want to expand. Here's the loan I think I need. What do you think?" That's a lot better than asking for the wrong loan at the wrong time in the wrong way. Your banker wants you to succeed and knows (if he or she is any good) that there's a high correlation between asking for (and heeding) professional advice and making a small business grow profitably.

Bankers hate surprises. If you face a problem, let your banker know immediately. Don't wait until it's a Friday night "gimme a loan or I go broke" issue. Let your banker work with you. Your banker's job is lending money and protecting depositors' assets. If your proposal is sound, you'll get your loan. If it isn't sound, you shouldn't. And if you disagree with your banker, be prepared to back up your renewed application with facts.

Establish more than one banking relationship. Spread the risk. Don't be dependent on one banker. Bankers move, retire, get promoted, leave banking, and have squabbles with the loan review committee. Plus, a line of credit may have to be paid out for ninety days each year. If you have two banks, you use both, keep both happy, satisfy the bank examiners, and have surplus credit available if you need it.

▶ Your Banker

Bankers are risk averse by training and temperament. They can't take the kinds of risks a venture capitalist or private investor might; that isn't their job. They tend to shun startups. They hate surprises. This leads to misunderstandings between small business owners and bankers. Small business owners, actual or prospective, have to learn that the relationship between them and their bankers should be businesslike. It certainly should not be hostile or antagonistic or demeaning, yet often is perceived that way. Make sure you cultivate bankers for their advice and support, have more than one bank, and be prepared to ask why credit is denied before getting angry.

5

What Do Potential Investors Want?

Investments come in two broad categories: credit and equity. Small businesses rely far more on credit than on equity. Bank loans are important, as are trade credit and leases of various kinds. Asset-based loans, such as loans against accounts receivable, play a role. Equity investment after startup depends largely on performance. If the business is profitable and needs capital to grow, the business can attract both inside investors (current owners and management) and outside investors. It can also generate capital from operations, and should, but that is only indirectly an investment.

Lenders look for the return of their capital plus interest. Investors look for return of capital, significant gains, plus in some cases, social returns. Investors range in sophistication from individuals with little business sense to the most experienced and cold-blooded venture capitalists.

Who Invests in Small Businesses Besides Banks?
You

You have to invest your personal savings and assets in your business before other investors will risk their capital. Your investment shows your belief in the business model and a willingness to accept the risks and rewards that your business generates. You should be the most cautious of all investors: you face personal, financial, career, and family risks, while other investors only risk capital. (Fortunately small business owners and other entrepreneurs are willing to barge ahead anyway. Otherwise there would be no new enterprises.)

What do you want? If you're like most people, you want a profitable business that affords a living first, with the possibility of significant capital gains second. Perhaps you have a vision of establishing a family business or a fortune.

You can raise cash from your savings and other investments, from the sale of assets (such as a boat or a car or art), home equity, or refinancing a major asset such as a house. You might have an insurance policy with cash value. After conferring with your accountant for possible tax consequences, you can tap retirement assets such as your 401(k) or IRAs. People have been known to use credit cards, but that route is expensive and risky.

Friends and Family

These are people who essentially invest in you. This has good and bad consequences. They want you to succeed (all investors want this) but if you don't they are not likely to hound you. It's a good idea to document their investment: Do they want interest on their investment or are they willing to let their capital stay with you until such time as you can cash out? Do they want part ownership? Do they want some say in the management of the business or are they willing to be passive investors?

The more you understand their wants, the better. Hidden agendas have wrecked many a growing business and even more relationships. Yes, friends and family are more willing to invest in your business than outside investors.

There are compelling legal and tax reasons to spell out the terms of the investment. Is their investment a loan to be repaid? What are the terms? Or is it an equity investment that gives them partial ownership? The IRS has been known to impute interest income to people who have informally loaned money to a small business.

SBA

The SBA has two main functions. First, it provides a wealth of free and low-cost advice to small business owners through publications, its Web site, trainings, seminars, and workshops. Second, it guarantees bank loans, principally through the 7(a) program.

What it doesn't do is provide direct investments or grants to small businesses. While there are a few programs on the books that purport to do this, they aren't funded—so don't waste energy pursuing them.

The SBA's mission is to help small businesses prosper. It won't back just any loan application; the applicant has to have a good chance of success. The SBA doesn't want to squander its resources on high-risk ventures, so in many ways it operates with the mindset of a careful banker.

The loan guarantees can make a difference between qualifying for a bank loan or not. The SBA can guarantee up to 85 percent of the principal, thus limiting the bank's exposure to loss.

Who's eligible? If you're unable to secure traditional bank financing, you are probably eligible. Go to the SBA Web site (sba.gov) to see if you qualify for any of the specialized SBA programs. This Web site has been greatly improved and is worth a visit, if only to get an idea of what the SBA can provide.

Your Business

Your profitable business should generate capital. This isn't a speedy process by any means, but over time it's the major source of capital for growth. For a short-term source of funds you might sell assets (equipment that you don't use, for example) or refinance assets. You might be able to sell a major asset to a leasing company (see below) and arrange to lease it back, thus enjoying use of the asset at a lower monthly cost.

Factors

Factors are big players in some industries. A factor will buy some or all of your receivables, either with recourse or without, and take over the collection of those receivables. The advantage to you is immediate cash. The downside is that this is an expensive mode of financing. The factor's interest is in establishing a continuing relationship with your business—repeat business in which they get to know and under-stand the rhythms of your sales and collection cycle.

Trade Credit

Trade credit is another major source of financing. Your suppliers want to continue to sell you their products and services, and if you a. are profit-able, and b. have a good credit history, they may be willing to extend terms to you. New businesses have a tough time getting trade credit, but once up and running you'll find this a valuable part of your financing plan.

Leasing Companies

Leasing companies range all the way from banks to manufacturers' internal leasing programs. Think of car leases—the leasing company owns the asset and gets the depreciation on it, which makes it possible for you to enjoy the use of the asset at a lower monthly cost than you would otherwise.

What gets leased? You name it: airplanes, railroad boxcars—equip-ment of all kinds.

Angels and Venture Capitalists

Angels and venture capitalists play an interesting role in financing small businesses. Authors like to include them in financing books be-cause angels and VC investors are exciting. However, their role in small business is tiny. Consider this factoid: Of the 750,000 new businesses that spring up each year, only 900 will get the attention (let alone the cash) of these investors. That works out to about one tenth of 1 percent, concentrated in high tech, medical, and big media industries.

That said, angels (individual investors, sometimes ad hoc groups of individual investors) provide seed capital for small businesses with significant growth potential. They tend to invest in areas where they have experience (doctors in medical software, for example). They invest through loans, direct equity, or a combination, such as convertible loans. They want to get their money back, of course, and want to get a good rate of return on their capital, but often have other motives than purely finan-cial. Some want to help their community, others want to encourage the coming generation of entrepreneurs, and some just want to keep busy.

Venture capital firms invest to make money. If you don't have a blowout technology or a huge potential secured by a proprietary lock on some important process, they'll ignore you.

Part Two

▼

The Financial Statements

Income Statement,
Balance Sheet,
Statement of Cash Flows

The Three Basic Financial Statements

The three basic financial statements are the **Balance Sheet** (also called the **Statement of Position**), the **Income Statement** (also called **Profit & Loss** or less formally the **P&L**), and the **Statement of Cash Flows** (CF). These compilations of financial information are tightly integrated. Changes in any one of them will affect one or both of the others. This relationship is examined in Chapter 12.

Financial Statements Are Tools

The format of financial statements has evolved to make comparisons and analysis easier and more helpful than would be the case with non-formatted financials. As with any tool, constant use and practice will sharpen your skills.

You don't have to be a bookkeeper or accountant to use financial statements. All you have to do is understand what they are about: They make large amounts of very detailed information about your business available. They make management easier and more effective. Your balance sheet shows what you own and what you owe. Your P&L shows whether you're making a profit or not. The Statement of Cash Flows provides a summary of the cash flows over the same period covered by the P&L.

The Balance Sheet

The balance sheet is the simplest of the financial statements (see "A Simplified Balance Sheet Format" on the next page). It gives you a snapshot of the condition of the business as of a given date. It is called a balance sheet because by definition:

▶ **Assets = Liabilities + Net Worth**

That's it. Assets (what you own) always equal the sum of the liabilities (what you owe) plus net worth.

Another way to put this:

▶ **Net Worth = Assets – Liabilities**

See Chapter 9 for a more detailed treatment of the Balance Sheet.

Current Assets are listed in order of decreasing liquidity: cash is cash (including deposit accounts), immediately available, while securities have to be sold, receivables converted to cash, all the way down to semi-liquid assets such as inventory which have to be sold to generate cash. Fixed Assets are those illiquid assets used to keep the business going: land, plant, equipment, and so on.

Similarly, Current Liabilities are listed in order of immediacy: Payables are due now, accrued expenses perhaps next month, current portion of long-term debt due within the year. Long-term Liabilities are those due more than a year out.

Net Worth is the difference between Total Assets and Total Liabilities. It's a derived figure, always equal to Total Assets minus Total Liabilities.

Items on the Balance Sheet

▶ **Current Assets** include cash, government securities, marketable securities, notes receivable (other than from officers or employees), accounts receivable, inventories, prepaid expenses, and any other item that will or could be converted to cash in the normal course of business within one year.

TABLE

▶A Simplified Balance Sheet Format

Name of Business

Date (month, day, year)

Balance Sheet

Assets

Current Assets		$_____
Fixed Assets	$_____	
Less Accumulated Depreciation	$_____	
Net Fixed Assets		$_____
Other Assets		$_____
Total Assets		$_____

Liabilities

Current Liabilities	$_____	
Long-Term Liabilities	$_____	
Total Liabilities:		$_____
Net Worth (total assets minus total liabilities)		$_____
Total Liabilities and Net Worth		$_____

▶ **Fixed Assets** include land, plant, equipment, leasehold improvements, and other items that have an expected useful business life measured in years.

▶ **Depreciation** is applied to those fixed assets that (unlike land) will wear out. This item has sizable tax consequences. The fixed asset value of a depreciable item is shown as the net of the cost of the item minus accumulated depreciation.

▶ **Other Assets** include intangible assets such as patents, copyrights, exclusive use contracts, and notes receivable from officers and employees.

▶ **Current Liabilities** include accounts payable, notes payable, accrued expenses (wages, salaries, withholding tax, FICA), taxes payable, current portion of long-term debt, and other obligations coming due within one year.

▶ **Long-Term Liabilities** include mortgages, trust deeds, intermediate and long-term bank loans, and equipment loans (all of these net of the current portion of long-term debt, which appears as a current liability).

▶ **Net Worth**, sometimes called *owner's equity*, can be broken down into owner's equity, retained earnings, and other equity.

You should provide displays of any extraordinary item (for example, a schedule of payables). Contingent liabilities such as pending lawsuits should be included in the footnotes. Changes of accounting practices would also be mentioned here.

The Income Statement or Profit & Loss (P&L)

The P&L is more like a movie than a still photo (see "A Simplified Income Statement Format" on the next page). It is designed to show what has happened in the business over a set period. The format always should include the dates covered by the statement. The standardized format is important. It makes the comparison with prior years' experience (or with other companies' experience) much easier.

The P&L shows whether the business has been profitable (or unprofitable) over the past period.

The basic shape of the P&L:

▶ **Net Sales – Total Expenses = Profit (Loss)**

This basic format is made more useful by expanding (and limiting) its component parts. A P&L for a small business might take half a page, while a Fortune 500 P&L would make up a small book. As always, keep it simple. An overly complicated P&L will only confuse you.

Items on the Income Statement

▶ **Net Sales** covers gross sales less returns, allowances, and discounts.

▶ **Cost of Goods Sold** includes cost of inventories.

▶ **Gross Margin** comprises net sales – cost of goods sold. This represents the gross profit on sales without taking indirect costs into account.

▶ **Operating Expenses** include the costs that, together with *other expenses*, must be met no matter what the sales level may be. The order in which they are stated isn't important. Thoroughness is. If some costs are trivial, lump them together under a head-

▶ A Simplified Income Statement Format

Net Sales		$_____
Cost of Goods Sold	$_____	
Gross Margin	$_____	
Operating Expenses	$_____	
Salaries and Wages	$_____	
Payroll Taxes and Benefits	$_____	
Rent	$_____	
Utilities	$_____	
Maintenance	$_____	
Office Supplies	$_____	
Postage	$_____	
Automobile and Truck	$_____	
Insurance	$_____	
Legal and Accounting	$_____	
Depreciation	$_____	
Other Expenses	$_____	
Interest	$_____	
Total Expenses	$_____	
Profit (Loss) Pre-Tax		$_____
Taxes	$_____	
Net Profit (Loss)		$_____

ing of "miscellaneous" but be prepared to break them out if the miscellaneous totals more than an arbitrary 1 percent of net sales.

▶ **Other Expenses** include non-operating expenses. The most common is interest expense. It's helpful to display your interest expense in some detail to both highlight the cost of money and to provide easy access to information used for ratio analysis.

▶ **Total Expenses** = Operating Expenses + Other Expenses.

▶ **Profit (Loss) Pre-Tax** = Gross Margin – Total Expenses. This is the tax base, the figure on which your tax will be calculated.

▶ **Taxes:** Consult your accountant.

▶ **Net profit (loss)** = Profit (loss) pre-tax – Taxes. This represents the success or lack thereof of your business. There are three ways to make this figure more positive: increase gross margin, decrease total expenses, or both.

Part One

Statement of Cash Flows

All publicly owned corporations have to include the Statement of Cash Flows in their annual reports. Other businesses, particularly small privately held businesses, seldom provide it. For budgeting purposes the cash flow *pro forma* is a better tool (see Chapter 23).

The Statement of Cash Flows shows how changes in the balance sheet and income accounts affected cash and cash equivalents for the reported period. This gives you a handle on future cash needs and a way to measure cash flow against estimates and other companies' performances.

The basic shape of the Statement of Cash Flows:

▶ **Cash from Operations + Cash from Investing + Cash from Financing**

TABLE

▶ **An Example of the Statement of Cash Flows Format**

Cash Flow from Operations		
Net profit		$ _____
Depreciation		$ _____
Changes to operating assets and liabilities:		
Accounts receivable	$ _____	
Inventory	$ _____	
Accounts Payable	$ _____	
Accrued Expenses	$ _____	
Net cash provided by operations		$ _____
Cash flows from investing activities:		
Additions to property, plant, and equipment		$ _____
Net cash from financing activities:		
Repayment of long-term debt		$ _____
Net cash provided (used)		$ _____

Together, the three financial statements tell a complete story. Taken individually, the statements provide only part of the story. For example, you could be making a profit but running out of cash. You need all three to get the complete story of what cash came in, where it went, and what changes have been made in the balance sheet.

7

Where Do the Numbers Come From?

The numbers in the financial statements aren't random. They're compiled from the numerous transactions that your business is involved in. Cash is invested, and cash is spent to purchase inventories or services, salaries, or taxes. Profits are generated, losses incurred. Loans are taken and repaid. Credit is extended to customers; customers repay these credits.

Remember the old computer saying "Garbage in, garbage out"? Good bookkeeping is based on accurate, timely data entry—and good bookkeeping is the basis of financial management and acceptable accounting.

If your small business is typical, one person is responsible for both finance (managing the company's financial resources) and accounting (recording and reporting all of its financial transactions). As your company grows, these functions will probably be separated, with accounting responsible for preparing reports, choosing and using accounting software, processing the flow of paperwork that documents

KEY INFO

▶ **The Bookkeeping Cycle**

Transactions (economic events)

↓

Entered into journals (sales, for example)

↓

Compiled in the General Ledger's Chart of Accounts

↓

Chart of Accounts compiled into the monthly finacial statements (the P&L, the balance sheet, statement of cash flows)

the transactions, and recording and maintaining the general ledger. That's a lot of work. Fortunately, due to the magic of double entry bookkeeping and your use of accrual accounting (see next chapter), a high degree of accuracy is almost guaranteed.

The structure of double entry systems is deceptively simple: Total debits must equal total credits. On a daily basis, journal entries are made recording all transactions the company is engaged in: sales and cash receipts, purchases, and other disbursements. These transactions are compiled in the general ledger monthly. Any adjusting entries are made (to cover matters such as depreciation and amortization, reduction of loan principal, dividends, and changes in net worth, for example). The Balance Sheet and Profit & Loss are built up from the information contained in the general ledger. At the end of the year (or other accounting period), the accounts are summarized and balanced and the cycle begins again.

Some economic historians maintain that the invention of double-entry bookkeeping had as great an impact on history as the invention of the printing press. If the accounts don't exactly balance, an error has been made, and can be quickly located without reconstructing the entire set of books. This is the standard on which the other systems are based. Your accountant will be thoroughly familiar with the ins and outs of this kind of bookkeeping system, and will help you understand the flow of information through it. You don't have to become an accountant to use and understand it.

You may have more transactions than can easily be handled by a full double entry manual bookkeeping system. Fortunately, computerized accounting systems are more adaptable, less expensive, and more reliable than ever. The advantages of computerized systems are speed, ability to handle sizable amounts of data, and best of all, the ability to pull a balance sheet, P&L, or cash flow at any time.

The drawbacks are the vulnerability of such systems (unless you carefully make backups of data) and the time it takes to learn the ins and outs of the systems.

8

Accrual Accounting vs. Cash Accounting

The difference between a cash system and an accrual system is that in a cash system, revenues and expenses are booked when cash changes hands: a merchant sells a shirt for $24 and books a sale of $24 the same day. Accrual systems cover the lag between when a sale is booked and when payment is received. A magazine publisher sells a one-year subscription and receives $24 today, but books the sale in twelve increments of $2 per month, which has the effect of deferring income. Or the merchant sells a $24 shirt today and books the sale, but doesn't get paid until next month.

Why should you use accrual accounting? If you face a timing difference between recognizing revenues and receiving cash, you need to be on an accrual system. You sell a product or service today and get paid later, perhaps next month or next year. You incur an expense today and pay for it next week or next month. It's unlikely that you would pay cash for property, plant, or major equipment.

In cash accounting (think of managing everything with a checkbook), the assumption is that revenue is cash received and expenses cash paid. For all but the simplest operation, this distorts what actually happens. If you are on a cash accounting system, what can you do about receivables and payables that extend beyond the period? (The answer is an intricate web of adjustments—no fun for anyone.)

The key to accrual accounting is to match expenses with the revenues they generate. Accrual recognizes that revenue may be earned before or after payment is received, and expenses may be incurred before or after payment is made. Think of the magazine publisher who gets paid in advance. He gets $24 in cash today, but doesn't earn it (book the revenue) until later when he fulfills the subscription. Think of a contractor who receives one-third down, one-third on completion, and one-third thirty days after completion. You may prepay some expenses—you might purchase insurance, paying for a year in advance. Or you may buy a piece of property and erect a building on it—and pay for it over a period of years.

Depreciation

Enter *depreciation*, a method of spreading the cost of an income-producing asset (the plant and property) over its useful life. Remember that the idea is to match the expense with the revenues it produces.

The simplest form of depreciation is straight-line depreciation. Suppose you buy a machine for $10,000 and expect it to last for five years.

Year	Asset Value	Depreciation	Accumulated Depreciation
0	$10,000	$0	$0
1	8,000	2,000	2,000
2	6,000	2,000	4,000
3	4,000	2,000	6,000
4	2,000	2,000	8,000
5	0	2,000	10,000

The assumption here is that the asset is used up at an even rate, which is seldom the case. Hence the IRS allows accelerated depreciation, a method more exactly matching the depreciation of the asset to its age.

For example, the $10,000 machine might be depreciated as follows:

Year	Asset Value	Depreciation	Accumulated Depreciation
0	$10,000	$0	$0
1	7,000	3,000	3,000
2	4,500	2,500	5,500
3	2,500	2,000	7,500
4	1,000	1,500	9,000
5	0	1,000	10,000

Depreciation has significant tax implications. This is an area where your accountant should guide you. The IRS provides Accelerated Cost Recovery System (ACRS) guidelines to help ensure that your depreciation schedules are acceptable.

▶ Amortization

Amortization is depreciation of intangible assets such as goodwill over a period of year. Suppose you buy a business for more than its asset value. The excess, what you paid for the business minus the asset value, is considered to be goodwill and can be straight-line depreciated over fifteen years. Consult your accountant!

Valuing Inventory

The purchase and production costs of inventory present another set of problems: How does inventory get charged as costs in the period in which it is sold? Cost of Goods Sold, the cost of any inventory sold during the accounting period, is complex. Some inventory will be left over from prior periods. Some inventory will be sold in a future period. Once again, accrual accounting matches the expense of the inventory with the revenue it produces. As a practical matter, this can be expressed in a formula:

▶ **Cost of Goods Sold = Beginning inventory + Production – Ending inventory**

The tax problem for your accountant is to decide which method of valuing inventory to use. The three choices are LIFO (last in, first out), FIFO (first in, first out) and Average Cost.

KEY INFO

▶ You Need Accrual Accounting if...

▶ You use or extend credit (payables and/or receivables).

▶ You have to correct the timing of recording sales revenue and expenses.

▶ You have to record liability for unpaid expenses.

▶ You use depreciation.

9

The Balance Sheet or Statement of Position

The balance sheet is the most basic piece of financial information required for managing a business and for obtaining financing from a bank. You have to fill out a balance sheet for many trade suppliers. They want to know whether they can safely extend credit to you. Since better than 90 percent of small business financing comes from banks and trade, this is of major importance.

The balance sheet is even more important as a management tool. While most small business owners pull a balance sheet once a year to satisfy tax information requirements, those owners who want to control their business pull one quarterly or even monthly. The information gained by comparing one date to another can alert the owner to developing trends—good or bad—and show where some tightening up or expansion may be needed.

The balance sheet is densely packed information—and profits come from information. Each element on it can be "unpacked" to provide more detailed information. For example, Fixed Assets represents the sum of the values of all plant and equipment owned by the business. At another level, managing fixed assets is different in substantial ways from managing current assets. Knowing the age and condition of inventory or receivables is essential knowledge. Their value is volatile.

What should you look for in a balance sheet? Look for changes from one period to the next; relationship of Current Assets-to-Current Liabilities; relationship of Debt–to-Net Worth. Dates: the inventory of a retailer just before Christmas is different from the inventory figure in January. The net worth (or owner's equity) figure is meaningless in some regard. Few businesses are sold at book value (net worth) because so many value judgments are buried or concealed in the balance sheet. On the other hand, banks will not lend to negative net worth businesses without compelling reasons and strong and secure personal guarantees.

What value judgments lurk in the balance sheet? Some of the more obvious ones are method of depreciation, concealed market values of fixed assets, replacement costs (and/or reserves for replacement), age and condition of inventory and receivables, values placed on "goodwill" or other assets being amortized, condition of liabilities, and contingent liabilities buried in obscure footnotes. Experienced financial types can read a balance sheet the way most of us read a newspaper. Newspapers are hardly objective, however, and sometimes contain misleading, incomplete, biased, slanted, or stale information. Balance sheets can also be misleading. Ideally, the information is clean and reliable. In practice, it may not be.

An astute business owner wants the balance sheet (and other financial statements) to be as clean as possible. The value judgments are inevitable, but if they are properly documented (a legal requirement for publicly traded companies), you can understand and mitigate their effect on your decisions. Sharp bankers insist on this kind of documentation.

Why call it a "balance sheet"? The balance sheet "balances" the assets and liabilities/net worth of the business. By definition,

▶ **Total Assets = Total Liabilities + Net Worth**

But more to the point, it helps the owner/manager better understand how the various pieces of the business work together. The simplest financial model, the balance sheet can be used to see if the company can afford to expand, pay its bills, develop new markets, and so on.

A business has to have certain balances. Sales and production, for example, coexist in a certain tension. If one overpowers the other, disaster can result. You balance risk and reward. Keeping lean and staffing up to meet market demands. Financial caution and leverage for accelerated growth. Balanced management expertise is important. A business is composed of a number of systems (including sales, administration, finance, personnel, marketing), all of which have to be balanced.

Pro forma balance sheets are important. (*Pro forma* financial statements are formatted projections.) A projected balance sheet is used to show the impact of major investments or other financial changes on the condition of a business. You use these to see what the impact of a refinancing would be on the balance sheet for one big reason: bankers look to the balance sheet to determine Debt-to-Net Worth ratios. If these are out of line with their norms, you won't receive a loan. Although the cash flow pro formas will show the impact of new debt, changed sales levels, and so on more clearly, the balance sheet makes a good summary. Fast growth, which most small business owners welcome, brings substantial risk: too little capital leads to over-leveraging, which can eat up profits and shunt a growing business into bankruptcy. Since projecting a balance sheet is tricky, leave it to your accountant. It's best to be accurate when you present a proposal to your banker.

The Balance Sheet

The balance sheet displays what you own (the assets of the business) and what you owe (the liabilities). The difference between the assets and liabilities is the net worth of the business. The format of the balance sheet is rigid: Both assets and liabilities are listed in order of decreasing liquidity. The list of assets starts with cash and ends with the least liquid, fixed assets; liabilities start with those bills you must meet now and end with the most remote.

Running a business efficiently and profitably calls for attaining and maintaining a delicate balance between and among all of the balance sheet items. You need enough cash to meet current obligations, but not too much. Cash is not a productive asset. You can actually reduce your profits by paying bills too soon.

The ratios in Chapter 17 will help you gauge the shape of your business, *shape* being the relative size and composition of assets, liabilities, and net worth. Some guidelines (especially useful for new businesses) can be gleaned from the usual trade and industry sources. Others come from your past financial statements.

Once again, trends reveal what your business is doing. Is net worth increasing, decreasing, or stable from one year to the next? Net worth is driven by net profit from the P&L. Are assets increasing or decreasing? How does the shape stack up against industry and historic standards? The heart of financial management and control is measuring performances against standards.

Get monthly balance sheets. With a computerized accounting system, this is a trifling task; with a manual accounting system it may take an hour or so. An annual balance sheet to please the IRS and your bank is of no use in running your business: you get too little information too late.

The following example will be used in Chapter 11 and in sections III and IV.

TABLE

▶ **Example Balance Sheet**

Balance Sheet
Aardvark Inc.

		12/31/10	12/31/11
Current Assets			
Cash		$112,050	$97,950
Accounts receivable		$140,400	$150,000
Inventory		$225,450	$253,500
Prepaid expenses		$20,550	$28,800
Current assets total		**$498,450**	**$530,250**
Fixed Assets			
Property, Plant, and Equipment		$403,500	$495,000
Accumulated depreciation		-$103,950	-$127,500
Cost less depreciation		$299,550	$367,500
Intangible assets		$150,000	$167,250

Fixed assets total	$449,550	$534,750
Total assets	$948,000	$1,065,000
Liabilities		
Accounts payable	$80,250	$99,600
Accrued expenses payable	$31,050	$45,450
Income tax payable	$2,460	$4,950
Short-term notes payable	$90,000	$93,750
Total Current Liabilities:	$203,760	$243,750
Long-term liabilities		
Notes payable	$20,000	$21,250
Notes payable (long-term)	$40,000	$30,000
Bank loans payable	$0	$0
Deferred taxes	$50,000	$45,000
Other loans payable	$0	$0
Other long-term liabilities	$0	$0
Total Long-Term Liabilities	$110,000	$96,250
Total Liabilities	$313,760	$340,000
Net Worth:		
Retained earnings	$394,240	$485,000
Invested capital	$240,000	$240,000
Total Net Worth	$634,240	$725,000
Total Liabilities & Net Worth:	$948,000	$1,065,000

Items on the Balance Sheet

▶ **Current assets** are all assets that will be converted into cash within one year in the normal course of business; cash, on hand or in checking, savings, or other deposit accounts.

▶ **Accounts receivable** is money owed to the company by its customers. In this example, look at the CF pro forma. The receivables which turn to cash in February were generated in January, so accounts receivable in January will be approximately equal to cash from receivables in February. The correlation is not exact. There will always be some slippage from one period to the next, and forecasts (as often noted) are never 100 percent accurate.

▶ **Inventory** is carried at cost. Inventory accounts are complex for manufacturers and retailers and vary according to the schedules (LIFO or FIFO) used to value them. Your accountant will advise you on how to value inventory, as it has substantial tax implications.

▶ **Pre-paid expense** includes deposits, advances on salaries, etc.

▶ **Fixed assets** are long-term assets that a company owns and uses to produce income. They will not be converted into cash in less than a year.

▶ **Accumulated depreciation** includes fixed assets that are "written off" over their anticipated life according to methods set by the IRS. This is a non-cash expense, which reduces taxable income. The concept is that you use up depreciable assets at a predictable pace and should be able to expense them over that period. Let your accountant worry about this. It doesn't affect operations. Intangibles include goodwill, value of copyrights and patents, and so on. The depreciation of an intangible is called *amortization*.

▶ **Accounts payable** is what you owe other businesses except banks and a few others, which is broken out separately.

▶ **Accrued expenses payable** are expenses that you have incurred but not yet paid. Salaries and inventories make up the bulk of this figure.

▶ **Income tax payable** includes taxes due but not yet paid.

▶ **Current portion of long-term debt** is the amount you are obligated to pay this year (the next 12 months) to your bank. If you have financed plant, property, or equipment, the balance owed shows this as a long-term liability.

▶ **Short-term notes payable** includes interest.

▶ **Long-term liabilities** are obligations you have incurred that don't come due until the following year.

▶ **Notes payable** are notes due but not yet paid.

▶ **Bank loans payable** equals bank debt minus current portion of long-term debt.

▶ **Deferred taxes** are a liability that results from income that has been earned for accounting purposes but not for tax purposes.

- ▶ **Other loans payable** could be a loan from an officer of the company. This covers loans that have been made to the company and that it still owes, but not from a normal financing source.
- ▶ **Retained earnings** are arguably the most obscure portion of the Balance Sheet. They are the portion of net earnings (from the P&L) not paid out as dividends or otherwise distributed. This figure fluctuates from one period to the next as the company earns or loses money. The trend and pattern is important; the small fluctuations are not.
- ▶ **Invested capital** is money permanently invested in the business. If you sell stocks, this figure increases; if you repurchase stock, it decreases.
- ▶ **Net worth** is the book value of the business, not to be confused with market value, which is the amount an informed buyer would pay an informed seller in an arm's length transaction. Since:

- ▶ **Assets – Liabilities = Net Worth**

You have to increase assets and decrease liabilities to improve net worth. You will have a negative net worth if your liabilities exceed your assets, a condition bankers abhor. In most cases, bankers can't lend money to a business with a negative net worth.

Projected balance sheets aren't often used in small businesses, though occasionally an investor or banker will request one. If that happens, have your accountant prepare it (plus whatever other schedules are needed), because it gets tricky. The changes in the various Balance Sheet entries are driven by both the P&L and the cash flow: If sales go up, for example, your accounts receivable and accounts payable will usually rise as well. So will inventories and the various loans payable. Cash is forecast by the cash flow, but how you'll actually employ that cash requires further thought.

If this sounds complex, it is. Yet a projected balance sheet provides useful guidelines. Sit down with your accountant and go through an exercise in which you tie your goals (expressed in your projected P&L and cash flow) to an idealized balance sheet, then work backward to ascertain what steps are going to get you there.

The short-term use of your monthly balance sheet is simple: Observe the changes over time. Any radical departure should be traced back to its cause. If you have a set of balance sheet-related goals, track them, too. These include improving the cash position, turning receivables faster, and controlling inventory. Such goals are important because accounts receivable and inventories are the dominant asset accounts. Keeping payables under control is another operating goal, a key indicator worth tracking.

Short-term fluctuations in net worth are not of great concern, but the trend is. The Aardvark example has a comparison format. Compare your balance sheet from month to month or graph monthly changes. You will discover new and interesting patterns in your business, which will lead to improved forecasts and performance.

▶ Interrelationships

The three main financial statements are interrelated. Look at the progression from the P&L to the cash flow to the balance sheet. As you pay down an equipment loan, for example, several things happen:

- ▶ **P&L:** You incur interest expense and non-cash depreciation expense.
- ▶ **Cash flow:** Principal and interest disbursements are recorded.
- ▶ **BS:** Current portion of long-term debt is lowered; accumulated depreciation increases.

Changes ripple through the P&L, cash flow, and balance sheet in more subtle ways. The interrelations are established so a skilled accountant or auditor will pick up any fudged numbers. You don't have to be an accountant to use these statements, just versed enough to raise questions if the numbers don't add up or feel right. That ability comes from experience in looking at the numbers, comparing them to standards, and looking for the discrepancies.

10

The Income Statement or Profit & Loss

The Income Statement (or Profit & Loss Statement, P&L) shows how your business performs over a period of time, usually by month and for tax purposes for the fiscal year. Make sure that your P&L follows standard formats, but keep in mind that its purpose is to reflect your business. It's not being prepared for your CPA's convenience or to fit a computer program. You can always take the information from your P&L and reformat it to meet other needs. Your fundamental need is to have accurate information available when you need it. An overly detailed P&L will not meet your needs. You won't use it, for one thing. As part of information control, keep it simple.

Items on the P&L

(Numbers reference lines in the sample P&L on the next page)

[1]   **Total sales for the period.** This is an aggregate figure. You may want to break it down, or have a separate sales schedule that breaks it down to its specifics.

TABLE

▶ Sample Format for a P&L

P&L for the period:

[1]	Gross Sales/Revenues	$_____
[2]	Less Discounts and Returns	$_____
[3]	Net Sales/Revenues	$_____
[4]	Less Cost of Goods Sold	$_____
[5]	Gross Profit (or Gross Margin)	$_____
[6]	Other Income	$_____
[7]	Total Receipts	$_____
[8]	Operating Expenses	
	Salaries/wages	
	Payroll taxes	
	Benefits	
	...	
	Miscellaneous	
[9]	Total Operating Expenses	$_____
[10]	Other Expenses	$_____
[11]	Interest	$_____
[12]	Total Expenses	$_____
[13]	Profit (Loss) Pre-tax	$_____
[14]	Taxes	$_____
[15]	Net Profit (Loss)	$_____

[2]   **Discounts and returns.** Monitor for quality and sales practices. Sudden increases in these accounts flash a major warning. Fluctuations may merely be a function of sales level, but have to be checked to ensure continued quality and customer satisfaction.

[3]   **Net economic returns from sales.**

[4]   **Cost of Goods Sold (COGS).** Includes cost of purchasing inventory and direct sales costs (commissions, royalties, and direct labor). COGS is usually the largest variable expense. In manufacturing companies, this provides the first measure of operating efficiency, and would be fairly detailed. Your accountant will help you determine the right amount of detail.

[5]   **Gross margin.** Gross sales minus discounts and returns, COGS. Sometimes called gross profit.

[6]   **Non-operating income such as profit on the sale of a fixed asset.** These are usually non-recurring items: returns on investments, legal claims etc.

[7]   [7] **Total receipts** = [5] **Gross margin** + [6] **Other income**

[8]   **Operating expenses are the costs of doing business.** Most of these are fixed, others are semi-variable, and a few are variable. The order they are presented in is less important than the thoroughness. If some expenses are trivial, lump them together as Miscellaneous. If the Miscellaneous expenses exceed an arbitrary 1 percent of sales, be prepared to break them out.

▶ Operating Expenses

Some business owners prefer to loosely categorize the operating expense line items rather than present them alphabetically or by size.

For example:

- ▶ Payroll expenses (includes salaries, taxes, benefits)
- ▶ Space costs (includes rent, utilities, maintenance)
- ▶ Professional services (principally, legal and accounting)
- ▶ Marketing expenses (includes advertising, trade show attendance, training, promotional expenses)
- ▶ Amortization and depreciation

[9]   **The sum of all operating expenses.** This is highly predictable because small differences in [8] tend to balance out.

[10]   **These are non-operating expenses,** such as...

[11]   **Interest** is the most familiar non-operating expense and is such an important measure that it should be given a prominent display. You want to monitor this closely. So will your banker.

[13]   You get taxed on this amount.

[14]   Consult your accountant. Tax minimization is a job for a specialist, as there are more than 50,000 pages in the tax

codes. Don't waste your time trying to master them. You have a business to run.

[15]   **This is the bottom line.** It represents the success or failure of the business.

There are many ways to present the income statement. This presentation begins with net revenues. It also compresses most operating expenses into SG&A, shorthand for Sales, General, and Administrative expenses. This format is used in many corporate reports, usually with detailed footnotes to show how they are derived. The virtue of this for the casual investor is ease of comprehension. It highlights the big income and expense items, and while the professional investment analysts need to get down in the weeds to see all the details, such depth of analysis is beyond most of us.

 TABLE

▶ **Sample P&L**

Income Statement for Aardvark Inc.
January 1 through December 31, 2011

Sales revenue	$1,560,000
COGS	$1,014,000
Gross margin	$546,000
SG&A	$374,400
Depreciation	$23,550
Earnings before interest and income tax	$148,050
Interest expense	$16,350
Profit (Loss) Pre-tax	$131,700
Income tax	$52,440
Net income	**$79,260**

The following example is used in Chapter 11 and sections III and IV. It's a more revealing P&L than the one immediately above—and more useful for purposes of financial control and financing.

▶ Sample P&L, More Detailed

Income Statement for Aardvark Inc.

January 1 through December 31, 2011

		TOTALS		
Sales Revenue				
	Products	$1,561,350		
	Other	$0		
	Returns & allowances	–$1,350		
Net Revenue		**$1,560,000**		
COST OF GOODS				
	Beginning merchandise inventory	$225,400		
	Net purchases of merchandise	$1,042,100		
	Ending merchandise inventory	$253,500	16.25%	
Total COGS		**$1,014,000**	65.00%	
Gross Margin		**$546,000**	35.00%	
Operating Expenses				
	Salaries etc.	$283,650	18.18%	
	Rent & utilities	$24,000	1.54%	
	Insurance	$12,000	0.77%	
	Marketing & advertising	$30,000	1.92%	
	Travel	$8,000	0.51%	
	Meals & entertainment	$3,000	0.19%	
	Professional fees	$1,200	0.08%	
	Telephone	$6,000	0.38%	
	Equipment leases	$3,600	0.23%	
	Repairs & maintenance	$1,200	0.08%	
	Amortization & depreciation	$23,550	1.51%	
	Miscellaneous	$1,750	0.11%	
Total Operating Expenses		**$397,950**	25.51%	
Earnings Before Interest & Taxes		**$148,050**	9.49%	
	Interest expense	$16,350	1.05%	
Pretax Profit (Loss)		**$131,700**	8.44%	
	Federal taxes	$52,440	3.36%	
	State taxes		0.00%	
Net Profit (Loss)		**$79,260**	5.08%	

Note the percentages in the far right column. This common-sizes the data to make comparisons with companies in the same line of work, trade averages, and perhaps most importantly, with Aardvark's historical performance. One P&L doesn't reveal a whole lot about how well the business is performing, but a series of P&Ls covering several years is a vital piece of the financial information puzzle.

11

Statement of Cash Flows

The *Statement of Cash Flows* (SCF) shows how your business pays for its operations and future growth. It highlights the critical nature of cash flow—the flow of cash into and out of your company—over the reporting period, usually a year. SCF is used to determine your company's liquidity and solvency, indicate possible ways to improve cash flows in the future, and to show how changes in assets, liabilities, and equity affect cash over the course of the year.

To generate your SCF you need two balance sheets, one from the end of the previous year and one from the end of the current year, plus the P&L from the current year.

The SCF has three sections:

1. Cash flows from operating activities
2. Cash flows from investing activities
3. Cash flows from financing activities

The results from each section are added together to compute the net increase or decrease in cash flow for the firm.

SCF begins with net income and adjusts for changes in account balances that affect cash. It shows how changes in balance sheet accounts and income affect cash and cash equivalents.

The Basic Shape of the SCF

There are eight basic rules for SCF:

1. Decreases in non-cash current assets are added to net income.
2. Increases in non-cash current assets are subtracted from net income.
3. Increases in current liabilities are added to net income.
4. Decreases in current liabilities are subtracted from net income.
5. Non-cash expenses (depreciation and amortization) are added back to net income.
6. Revenues with no cash inflows are subtracted from net income.
7. Non-operating losses are added back to net income.
8. Non-operating gains are subtracted from net income.

 TABLE

▶ **Building the SCF**

Step 1:   Show changes in cash flow due to operations

Period ending	12/31/11
Net income	
Operating activities, cash flows provided by or used in:	
Depreciation and amortization	
Adjustments to net income	
Decrease (increase) in accounts receivable	
Increase (decrease) in liabilities (accounts payable, taxes payable)	
Decrease (increase) in inventories	
Increase (decrease) in other operating activities	
Net cash flow from operating activities	

Step 2:   Show changes in cash flow due to investing activities

Period ending	12/31/11
Investing activities, cash flows provided by or used in:	

Capital expenditures (plant, property, equipment)	
Investments	
Other cash flows from investing activities	
Net cash flow from investing activities	

Step 3: Show changes in cash flows due to financing activities

Period ending	12/31/11
Financing activities, cash flows provided by or used in:	
Dividends paid to stockholders	
Sale (repurchase) of stock	
Increase (decrease) in debt	
Other cash flows from financing activities	
Net cash flow from financing activities	

Step 4: Bring these together to determine the net increase (decrease) in cash over the year

Period ending	12/31/11
Net income	
Operating activities, cash flows provided by or used in:	
Depreciation and amortization	
Adjustments to net income	
Decrease (increase) in accounts receivable	
Increase (decrease) in liabilities (accounts payable, taxes payable)	
Decrease (increase) in inventories	
Increase (decrease) in other operating activities	
Net cash flow from operating activities	
Investing activities, cash flows provided by or used in:	
Capital expenditures (plant, property, equipment)	
Investments	
Other cash flows from investing activities	
Net cash flow from investing activities	
Financing activities, cash flows provided by or used in:	
Dividends paid to stockholders	
Sale (repurchase) of stock	
Increase (decrease) in debt	
Other cash flows from financing activities	
Net cash flow from financing activities	
Net increase (decrease) in cash and cash equivalents	

T ~~MORE~~

▶ **The Cash Flow Cycle**

It's helpful to be aware of the Cash Flow Cycle. You begin a business with cash (perhaps a modest amount), then:

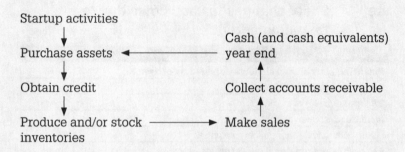

Startup activities
↓
Purchase assets ◀——————— Cash (and cash equivalents) year end
↓   ↑
Obtain credit   Collect accounts receivable
↓   ↑
Produce and/or stock ——————▶ Make sales
inventories

   This cycle repeats itself (except for startup activities, unless you include expansion as a startup) every year.

The Statement of Cash Flows shows how changes in the balance sheet and income accounts affect cash and cash equivalents for the reported period.

Other Helpful Ways to Think About SCF

There are four kinds of transactions to keep in mind:

1. Growth in accounts receivable increases profits but doesn't produce cash until later.
2. Accounts payable decreases profits but doesn't reduce cash until later.
3. Securing loans and investors puts cash in the bank but may or may not help profits until later.
4. Repaying debt or purchasing fixed assets (plant, property, equipment) takes cash but may or may not affect profits later.

SCF Adjustments

What adjustments should you make to arrive at the cash flow for the period under examination?

Chapter 11

Step 1: Operating Activities

1. Start with net income from the income statement.
2. Add back entries to expense accounts that don't represent cash flows (especially depreciation and amortization).

This equals cash flows before movements in working capital.

3. Add back or subtract changes in working capital as follows:
   a. An increase in current assets (excluding cash and cash equivalents) would be shown as a negative figure because cash was spent or converted into other current assets, thereby reducing the cash balance.
   b. A decrease in current assets would be shown as a positive figure, because other current assets were converted into cash.
   c. An increase in current liabilities (excluding short-term debt which would be reported in the financing activities section) would be shown as a positive figure since more liabilities mean that less cash was spent.
   d. A decrease in current liabilities would be shown as a negative figure, because cash was spent to reduce liabilities.

The net effect of the above would then be reported as cash provided by (used in) operating activities.

Step 2: Investing Activities

Subtract the increase in expenditures for plant, property, and equipment, a use of cash; add back a decrease, which would reflect a source of cash.

The same applies for intangible assets: an increase is a use of cash, a decrease, a source of cash.

Step 3: Financing Activities

1. Add back increases in short-term debt; subtract decreases in short-term debt.
2. Add back increases in long-term debt; subtract decreases in long-term debt.
3. Add in new capital (sales of stock, direct investment).
4. Subtract dividends or other distributions.

Step 4:   Calculating the Cash Flow

Add the results of the operating, investment, and financing activities. The data in the following example comes from Chapters 9 and 10.

▶ Statement of Cash Flows

Aardvark Inc.
Statement of Cash Flows for 2011

Cash Flow from Operating Activities		
Net income	$79,260	
Accounts receivable increase	(9,600)	
Inventory increase	(28,050)	
Prepaid expense increase	(8,250)	
Depreciation expense	23,550	
Accounts payable increase	19,350	
Accrued expenses payable increase	14,400	
Income tax payable increase	2,490	93,150
Cash flow from Investing Activities		
Expenditures for PP&E	(91,500)	
Expenses for intangible assets	0	(91,500)
Cash Flow from Financing Activities		
Increase in short term debt	3,750	
Decrease in long term debt	(10,000)	
New capital investment	0	(6,250)
Increase (Decrease) in cash during year		**(14,400)**
Cash balance start of year		112,050
Cash balance end of year		97,950

12

How the Financial Statements Interact

The three basic financial statements together form a dynamic system. Changes in the P&L cause changes in the balance sheet and SCF; changes in the balance sheet ripple over to the SCF and in some cases alter the P&L; changes in the SCF may impact the P&L and will alter the balance sheet. Knowing how these interactions work can help you make better use of your financial statements.

Changes in the balance sheet during the accounting period occasion changes in net income, which is reflected in the statement of cash flows.

It's easiest to start with the Balance Sheet.

First look at changes in the Current Assets (CA).

1. **Add decreases in non-cash CA back to net income.** Of particular interest are accounts receivable (AR), inventory, and prepaid expenses. If AR decreases, cash must have come in as people paid their invoices. If inventory decreases, products presumably have been sold.

2. **Subtract increases in non-cash CA from net income.** If AR increases, products have been sold but not yet paid for. If prepaid expenses increase, cash has been expended.

Now look at changes in the Current Liabilities (CL).

3. **Add increases in CL back into net income.** When notes payable increase, cash comes in.
4. **Subtract decreases in CL from net income.** When notes payable goes down, cash goes out (to pay down the note). The same reasoning applies to accounts payable, current portion of long-term debt, accrued expenses, and income tax payable.

Turn to the P&L to review the non-cash expenses and revenues.

5. **Add depreciation and amortization back into net income.** No cash has been exchanged. These are non-cash expenses.
6. **Subtract revenues with no cash inflow from net income.** These revenues appear in accounts receivable, but no cash has yet changed hands.
7. **Non-operating losses are added back into net income.** Examples of non-operating losses include write-down of an asset or losses from investments outside of the business.
8. **Subtract non-operating gains from net income.** These gains might come from the sale of a fixed asset (equipment, plant, or other property), writing up the value of an asset, or profits from investments.

Now look at the framework for figuring the Statement of Cash Flows. The first part covers operations.

Period ending	12/31/11
Net income	
Operating activities, cash flows provided by or used in:	
Depreciation and amortization	
Adjustments to net income	
Decrease (increase) in accounts receivable	

Increase (decrease) in liabilities (accounts payable, taxes payable)	
Decrease (increase) in inventories	
Increase (decrease) in other operating activities	
Net cash flow from operating activities	

Note that all of the information comes from the P&L and the beginning and ending balance sheets for the period covered.

Period ending	12/31/11
Investing activities, cash flows provided by or used in:	
Capital expenditures (plant, property, equipment)	
Investments	
Other cash flows from investing activities	
Net cash flow from investing activities	

Cash Flows from investing reflect capital expenditures in 7 and 8 above.

Period ending	12/31/11
Financing activities, cash flows provided by or used in:	
Dividends paid to stockholders	
Sale (repurchase) of stock	
Increase (decrease) in debt	
Other cash flows from financing activities	
Net cash flow from financing activities	

Financing activities are defined by changes in the Owners' Equity (or Net Worth) section of the balance sheets. Sale of stock leads to cash inflow; repurchase of stock to cash outflow. Increase in debt brings in cash; repayment to cash outflows.

There's nothing magic about this. It does compel careful attention to the movement (amount and timing) of cash in and out of the business, and that's a good thing.

Part
Three

▼

Reading and Analyzing Financial Statements

Ratios, Comparisons, Common-Sizing, and More

13

What is Financial Analysis?

Financial analysis is a structured way to look at a company's financial statements. The two main reasons to do this are 1. to make a determination of whether to buy or sell the company's publicly listed stocks or bonds and 2. to understand how the business is performing (looking at the past, the present, and the future), identify strengths to build on and weaknesses to shore up, analyze the information, and if necessary, adjust business practices going forward.

The first reason is somewhat beside the point for this book, but is an important reason for any investor to pay attention to publicly available financial information. While it's unlikely that you'll discover information that Financial Analysts (capitals deliberate) well-trained in poring over Google's financials overlooked, you may want to know what those Financial Analysts mean when they write about Google's stocks and use terms such as *leverage* and *return on investment*. Financial analysts are highly paid, experienced professionals who do nothing but analyze publicly owned stocks and bonds.

The second reason for financial analysis is more important for small business owners who are asking themselves the two key management questions: Should I invest more in my business? Or should I disinvest?

Your financials, properly grounded in current and anticipated economic and competitive contexts, contain the answers.

Financial analysis will help you plan your company's future. It bases the numbers on realistic annotated assumptions—the footnotes that accompany the financials—and lets you play what-if, comparing different scenarios for your business's future. Playing what-if is a lot less expensive than plunging ahead only to discover that you're on a seriously wrong course. What if your sales double over the next year? What if the economy crashes? What if you acquire that competing store? What are the economic consequences of any of these scenarios?

Financial analysis is deeply involved in setting and evaluating budgets, built on projected P&Ls and the cash flows pro forma. Almost every business has built-in momentum based on its past performance. Unless there's good reason to believe otherwise (perhaps your business is in a turnaround situation, or has just closed on a major piece of financing to purchase a competitor), the near future will pretty much reflect past performance. Changes are suggested by reviewing past performance and considering how plans for the next one to five years will affect your budgets. Are these changes affordable? Wise? Once again, financial analysis can help you make good decisions.

You'll use your budgets, tested by financial analysis, to monitor performance and make sure that your financial goals are being met. There's a cascading effect here: You used financial analysis to understand your company's past performance, plan for its future, and set budgets. While budget deviation analysis isn't part of financial analysis, it is based on your understanding and planning.

Financial analysis will help you improve all of the financial details of your business. For example, do you know how many days' inventory you have on hand? How about receivables? How does this affect cash flow?

Many questions. Many answers. In no particular order, you use financial analysis to assess your company's liquidity (ability to meet current obligations), solvency (ability to meet long-term obligations), coverage (ability to service debt), leverage (exposure to risk and vulnerability to business downturns), and operations (measure of management performance, including profitability). It can also help you determine your company's stability—its ability to stay in business over the long haul.

14

The Importance of Context

One definition of *context* is "the interrelated conditions in which something exists or occurs." Another is "the whole situation, background and environments relevant to the activity." Yet another is "the set of facts or circumstances that surround a situation or event."

Your business operates in a variety of contexts that affect its performance. Some are within your control, some are not. Some are relevant, some are not. Better beware—you can dodge what you can see coming, but if you aren't alert you can be blindsided.

Some contexts to be aware of are listed below. Some will be useful to you, others won't be. Use your best judgment. But know, please, that bankers and other investors are intensely interested in your marketing and product plans, and make their investment decisions with their perception of your understanding of these wider contexts.

Economic Factors

The business cycle, alternating between boom and bust, has an obvious impact. The deep recession of 2008–2010, for example, resulted in sharp contractions in almost every industry. It was particularly hard on the construction industry and its allied industries. Some regions of the country suffered more than others; the regional and local economies differ considerably.

National or international economic conditions influence the availability of investment money, availability of bank funds, and how much your customers can spend on your products. Regional and local economic conditions may trump the larger economies: loss of a major industry can devastate a local economy while the national economy is booming.

The solution: Keep reading *The Wall Street Journal* or other business publications. Keep reading local papers, chat up your banker friends, and talk with other local business owners. Go to trade shows

T MORE

▶ Life Cycles

The one constant, as Heraclitus noted 2,500 years ago, is change. Businesses, products, services, industries, even countries go through the cycle of:

introduction ⟶
     growth ⟶
         maturity ⟶
            decline

The introductory phase is full of uncertainties and challenges. Once established, there is a period of growth, sometimes very rapid, and sometimes slow but steady. At some point the growth stops, and a period of indefinite length called maturity sets in. In this phase there is little change and a lot of "business as usual" until the last stage, decline, sets in and the business, product, or industry vanishes or implodes.

The life cycle is used as an explanatory tool. It has limitations of subjectivity and uncertainty, but it does help organize analysis of the business, product, or industry.

(again!) to learn about what's going on in other parts of the country (also helpful for spotting trends and new products).

Age and Stage of Your Business

No business lasts forever (though they may last for a long time). Where your business stands on its (probable) life cycle has implications for your forecasts. New businesses are hard to predict. Their history is short and if they are growing, questions of capital needs have to be addressed. Growth is expensive and often seen as risky by bankers. Mature businesses are the easiest to forecast. Declining businesses merit careful analysis: the transition may suddenly accelerate, you might decide to sell out and retire, or your bank may pull the plug.

The age and skills of your employees and management will have an impact, too: Is a key employee about to retire? Are the remaining skills adequate to the challenges of the near future?

Industry Factors

Industries have life cycles, too. Look at the steamship industry: It was highly innovative in 1802 when William Symington in England built the *Charlotte Dundas*. Robert Fulton opened the markets in the early 1800s and for over a century the steamship ruled the waves. Technological change ultimately led to the decline of the industry, which now exists mainly for hobbyists.

Consider the ups and downs of the railroad industry. A decline doesn't always mean the elimination of an industry. From the 1870s until shortly after World War II the railroads were king (or queen). The advent of the interstate highway and the proliferation of diesel trucks led to the decline of the railroad industry. And now it's coming back, as evidenced by high-speed rail proposals, mounting ecological concerns here and abroad about the trucking industry, new alliances with container ships, and a host of other factors.

Want some examples? Stem cell research and genetics research are in an early phase of what promise to become major medical businesses, much like stents were for Boston Scientific twenty years ago. Telecommunications, computers, and information technologies (Google, anyone?) are growing exponentially. Cell phones are endemic, approaching maturity but hugely successful. The computer chip industry is mature, as are Big Box stores, while newspapers and mass magazines are beginning to slide. Tobacco, steel, film camera, and video rental stores are in decline. Typesetting is an almost extinct skill, replaced by the computer. Interestingly, mass transit and railroads seem to have found new life and may be considered to be somewhere between introduction and growth.

Product Factors

There is a spectrum here, ranging from introduction of products through growth, to maturity, and to decline. Where your business is on this scale matters. If your inventory is composed of declining products...

The products and services that represent the industries on the life cycle above mirror the industries. Sales at Walmart are flat. It's hard to find a local store that processes 35mm film. Polaroid has almost vanished. Product (and industry) life cycles are carefully covered in trade association publications because they are so important to understanding what's going on.

▶ Ways to Avoid Product Obsolescence

1. Do you have new or improved products or services in the pipeline? Or are you planning to continue with what you currently have?
2. Are there substitutes available for your products?
3. Can you come up with new applications for your products?

Marketing Factors

Are your markets growing, stable, or slowing? Markets have a life cycle, too.

Is your market share growing? Shrinking? Stable? Is new or heightened price competition appearing? (Unexpected changes in pricing can blow up your sales forecasts.)

Marketing factors exert a big impact on the validity of your forecasts. A Boston Consulting Group matrix is one way to view your products (or product lines).

The stars use lots of cash but spin off large amounts of cash. Cash

▶ Boston Consulting Group Matrix

Stars, with high market shares in fast-growing markets	Question marks, with low market share of a high-growth market
Cash cows, with high market share of a slow or declining market	Dogs, with a low share of low-growth market

cows generate cash and profits and don't require a lot of investment. Dogs are bad news: get rid of them, and be leery of "But we can turn this one around!" Question marks have high cash demands and low cash delivery, so raise the tough questions of invest, divest, or stop investing in them and take whatever cash they can generate.

Technological Factors

The past decade has seen breathtaking technological advances in communications, medicine, and other fields. Look at the plight of newspapers due to the advent of Craigslist.org! The venerable cash cow for newspapers, the classified advertising section has been gutted. Or look at the sharp and unexpected decline of the traditional camera and film markets due to digital cameras. Textbook publishers are panicked at the very real threat of digitized textbooks.

You must keep an eye on the technologies affecting your industry. You may not have a solution (newspapers don't) but you can take precautions, change your business model, and revamp your thinking.

Other Matters To Take Into Context

- ▶ Take politics into your thinking.
- ▶ How are your suppliers doing? What are they hearing?
- ▶ Have you built seasonality into your thinking?

The key: Context matters.

15

Basic Financial Analysis Tools

Historical Financial Statements

Compelling reasons to keep business records include:

▶ Businesses have a momentum that's difficult to alter.
▶ Past performance is an excellent—though not infallible—
  guide to future performance.
▶ Sales patterns established over years make planning easier and
  more accurate.
▶ Historical records provide substantiation for projections.
▶ Bankers require them.

What historical financials should you retain? The most important are tax returns and operating statements. All tax returns should be saved for a minimum of seven years, although it's safer to save them forever just in case. The cost of storage is trivial compared to the cost of reconstructing tax returns from old bank records, old files covered with dust in a storage facility, other companies' incomplete records, and so forth. In IRS matters, the burden of proof is on you. Old operating statements (annual P&Ls, balance sheets, other records) can keep a business focused, heighten knowledge of its markets, and hint at ways to improve performance. Their informational and archival value is significant.

Why save these things? Prudence and profit. Prudence says save them to guard against IRS and other potential claimants. Your accountant or tax advisor can give you some guidelines here, your attorney other guidelines. While you won't want to save everything forever, you will want to save all records for a minimum of seven years. Profit says you can learn from them—and when you decide to sell your business, you may be able to justify a higher price by showing how, for example, the business is stable and low risk, retains customers for years, and has a developing profitability rate. And so on. Unsubstantiated claims in these areas don't get capitalized as "good will." They get knocked off the purchase price.

Common-sized historical statements provide a measure of improvement. A common-sized P&L expresses all line items in terms of percentage of annual sales. A common-sized balance sheet expresses all balance sheet items as percentages of total assets. This facilitates comparisons from one year to the next and helps highlight long-term trends. All businesses should generate these; they provide a report card which answers the owner's most common question: "How'm I doing?"

Comparisons of many kinds are at the heart of financial analysis. Some of the more important comparisons are:

▶ **Comparison of the company's performance with its own historical performance**
▶ **Comparison with trade averages**
▶ **Comparisons with publicly available measures such as the** *Financial Studies of the Small Business* **published annually by Financial Research Associates, Orlando FL** (covers 30,000 small businesses in 70 industries, all businesses with capitalization under $1 million)
▶ **Comparisons with future performance such as proposed budgets, forecasts, and pro formas**

Use a form such as one of the following to track performance.

▶ Performance Tracking

Current	Last Year	Y-2	Y-3	Projected
Revenues				
Gross Margin				
Operating Net				
Profit (Loss)				
Net Worth				

Current	Trade or Industry Ratios	Y-1	Y-2
Current Ratio			
AR Turnover			
Inventory Turnover			
Debt-to-Net Worth			
EBIT/Net Worth			

EBIT is Earnings Before Interest and Taxes, a measure of the operating earnings of the business.

Trend Analysis

Spotting and understanding trends is an important part of financial analysis. This rests on the tendency of businesses to maintain course over time. Some specific trends worth following:

- ▶ Revenues
- ▶ Margins
- ▶ Costs
- ▶ Accounts Payable and Accounts Receivable
- ▶ Inventories
- ▶ Profits (Losses)

These are examined in subsequent chapters.

Ratios

Ratios make use of the information contained in the financial statements and other reports. The key ratios are grouped together as follows:

▶ **Liquidity ratios are used to indicate your firm's ability to meet current obligations on time.** An illiquid firm has difficulty paying its bills and needs more capital, better management, or both.

▶ **Coverage ratios measure the company's ability to service debt—particularly bank debt.**

▶ **Leverage ratios measure exposure to risk and vulnerability to business downturns.**

▶ **Operating ratios provide a measure of management performance.**

KEY INFO

▶ Where to Find Trade Ratios

You can find an excellent list of industry financial and operating ratios at www2.lib.udel.edu/subj/bsec/resguide/indufina.htm. This is the University of Delaware Library. Don't forget to use your local research librarian in your quest for information!

MORE

▶ Gale's *Small Business Sourcebook*

Quoting the publisher:

In this annual two-volume annotated guide, you'll discover more than 340 specific small business profiles and 99 general small business topics; small business programs and assistance programs in the U.S., its territories, and Canadian provinces; and U.S. federal government agencies and offices specializing in small business issues, programs and assistance. Entries include (as appropriate and available) organization, institution, or product name; contact information, including contact name, address, phone, toll-free, and fax numbers; author/editor name, date(s), and frequency of publication; availability, including price; brief description of purpose, services, or content; company and/or personal e-mail addresses; and URL information.

This is highly recommended. You can probably find it in your library, or get it through inter-library loan.

16

Trend Analysis

Comparisons year-to-year and period-to-period yield valuable information. The year-end comparisons are helpful, but can conceal valuable seasonal or other shifts. One reason for the "rolling 12-month projection" is that comparing July 2010 to July 2011 (and so on) makes it easier to spot trends. Quarterly summaries yield other kinds of information, as a three-month period is long enough to smooth out aberrant monthly data and short enough to spot significant shifts.

Trend Analysis?

Trend analysis attempts to predict the future performance of a company or movement of a stock on the basis of past data.

For you, the owner of a small business, trend analysis is based on the idea that what has been a pattern in the past will—unless there's a significant change—continue in the future. Part of this is due to momentum: it takes time to change the way a company does business. Part is due to habit: you do many things without thinking about them, which allows you to get more done than you could otherwise.

For investors in the stock market, trend analysis is based on the idea that historical trading trends can give traders an idea of what may happen in the future. There are three types of trends: short-term, intermediate-term, and long-term.

Trend analysis is also used to predict a trend such as a bull market so that investors can ride that trend until data suggests a trend reversal (for example, bull market to bear market). Trend analysis is helpful because moving with trends, as opposed to against them, can lead to profits for an investor.

Less formally, in trend analysis you look for trends in the world around you, and then try to figure out what these trends might mean for your business. You already do this—you can't escape hearing about current economic trends—but if you look for trends more intentionally, chances are good that you will gain a step on your competition.

KEY INFO

▶ Trend Ratio Analysis

Trend ratio analysis is the comparison of the successive values of each ratio for a single firm over a number of years. The ratios are explained in the next chapter.

Ratio:	2008	2009	2010
Current Ratio	2.1	2.4	2.1
Fixed/Net Worth	1.3	1.7	1.2
EBIT/Interest	3.2	3.0	5.2
Profit Before Taxes/Net Worth	11.8	10.8	14.2

These are positive trends. Management is doing something right.

Be especially vigilant in looking for the following trends. Some are non-financial but have a lot of impact on your company's performance. Take notes—you'll use this information when you prepare your business plans and forecasts.

Business Trends

Check revenues, expenses, debt, and capital over the past few years. Is there a pattern? Ratio trend analysis is especially helpful. The ratios provide deeper insights into how the business is doing than you can glean from the financial statements alone.

Market Trends

What has been going on in your markets during the past few years? No market remains the same for long. It doesn't matter whether you're selling to individuals, other businesses, or government agencies. Your markets will change. Tastes, demographics, technologies, and products change. Remember that the aim of trend spotting is to enrich the context that your business plan and/or financing proposal will be written in. You want to be aware of both financial and non-financial trends. Look at the abysmal trends in the real estate market over the years 2007 through 2010. More positively, look at the rebound of US automakers over the same period.

Competitive Trends

One subset of the marketing arena involves the ever-changing nature of competitors. Attractive markets draw new competitors. Unattractive markets drive competitors away. What is going on with your competitors? Some things to do: Keep simple manila folders for each direct competitor, toss in clips of ads, notes, information about their size, profitability, market share, and so on. Then review the files periodically. This will give you a better feel for what your competitors are up to and what they will do in the near future.

Economic Trends

The economy (in the sense of the big picture) has been dismal for the past few years. As a result, banks have suffered and, of course, are more than happy to pass the suffering along to the small business community. When banks' balance sheets are weak, they won't make loans, or are more vigilant in screening loan proposals than they normally would be.

Current and Local Financial Trends

Small businesses operate locally. As a consequence there may be a disconnect between what is going on nationally and what is going on locally.

Trend Analysis Combines Financial and Non-Financial Data

The strength of trend analysis is that it is a mix of financial and non-financial information, another example of an enriched context for making decisions. If numbers alone could reliably predict the near future life would have fewer uncertainties.

▶ **It places the events of a single year in a long-term perspective and permits a company to follow changes over time.**

▶ **It incorporates benchmarks normally used by banks and other investors.** Is the economy reaching a turning point as measured by changes in gross economic measures such as Gross Domestic Product, or finer measures such as employment rates and foreclosure rates? The implications of such trends are worth spelling out.

▶ **It provides the framework for assembling and analyzing information about the business on a regular basis.**

▶ **This approach relies heavily on the determination and analysis of selected key trends.** The identification of one adverse trend, however, does not automatically represent fiscal decline. Some trends, which on the surface may appear adverse, may, after careful analysis, prove harmless. Moreover, the techniques involved are intended to provide an overview of the financial condition of your business. The results obtained from using these techniques are a good beginning point for analysis, not a conclusion.

The system cannot explain specifically why a problem is occurring, nor does it provide a single number or index to measure financial health. What it does provide are flags for identifying problems, clues about their causes, and time to take anticipatory action.

17

Ratio Analysis

Volumes have been written on ratios, but there are really only a handful that matter to most small business owners and managers. With a small set of ratios you can quickly identify where improvements are needed. As you run your business you juggle dozens of variables. Ratio analysis is designed to help you identify those variables that are out of balance.

Ratios taken singly can be misleading, but when compared to industry or other norms and followed over time to ascertain trends, they will be highly valuable. Ratios help you interpret the relationships of P&L and balance sheet figures and get maximum information from your financial statements.

Bankers and other investors love ratios. This fact alone makes ratio analysis important. If your Current Ratio, Acid Test, or Debt/Net Worth are out of whack with your banker's expectations, your business will be less bankable unless you can explain them.

Ratios are used *absolutely*, standing on their own as measures of your business at the time the information they are based on was compiled, and *relatively*, comparing performance to trade or industry standards (Financial Research Associates and others), to historical performance, or to other standards. Both uses are valuable. Keeping track of key ratios over a period of months or years is a powerful way to spot trends in the making.

Ratios are commonly categorized in four groups: Liquidity, Coverage, Leverage, and Operating.

Keep in mind that all of the following ratios are based on *when* your financial statements are calculated. This sensitivity to timing is a factor you should take into account. A retail store's balance sheet drawn up just before the Christmas season when inventory is high and accounts receivable are low will present a different picture than a balance sheet drawn up just after New Year's Day, when inventory will be low and accounts receivables high.

Liquidity Ratios

Use *liquidity* ratios to indicate your firm's ability to meet current obligations on time. An illiquid firm has difficulty paying its bills and needs more capital, better management, or both.

KEY INFO

▶ **Current Ratio**

$$\frac{\text{Total Current Assets}}{\text{Total Current Liabilities}}$$

Example

Current Ratio: $\dfrac{\$530{,}250}{\$243{,}750} = 2.2$

The current ratio is commonly used to measure ability to meet short-term debt. The rule of thumb is that this should be at least 2:1. This is because some of the assets involved (especially inventory) may take a while to turn to cash to meet current obligations in a timely way. The current ratio depends on the quality of the current assets. This is the most widely used single ratio. Its widespread use highlights the importance of maintaining liquidity.

▶ Acid Test (or Quick Ratio)

$$\frac{\text{Cash} + \text{Equivalents} + \text{Accounts Receivable}}{\text{Total Current Liabilities}}$$

Example

Acid Test: $\dfrac{\$97,950 + 150,000}{\$243,750} = 2.2$

This is a more precise measure of current liquidity. The rule of thumb calls for an acid test ratio of 1:1. A ratio lower than 1:1 indicates an unhealthy reliance on inventory or other current assets to meet short-term obligations. A higher acid test ratio may indicate excessive cash or lax collection efforts.

▶ Sales/Receivables

$$\frac{\text{Net Sales}}{\text{Accounts Receivable (Net)}}$$

Example

Sales/Receivables: $\dfrac{\$1,560,000}{\$150,000} = 10.4$

Sales-to-Receivables measures the annual turnover of receivables. Higher values indicate a shorter term between sales and cash collection. Lower values can indicate a collection problem due either to lax collection efforts or low-quality receivables. This ratio is affected by seasonality. If possible, use an average receivables figure rather than year-end to correct for seasonality. Using Aardvark's average receivables:

$$(140,400 + 150,000) / 2 = \$145,200$$

Example

Sales/Average Receivables: $\dfrac{\$1,560,000}{\$145,200} = 10.7$

▶ Days' Receivables

$$\frac{365}{\text{Sales/Receivables}}$$

Example

Days' Receivables: $\dfrac{365}{10.7} = 34 \text{ days}$

This measures the average time in days that accounts receivables are outstanding. This ratio is subject to the same caution concerning seasonality as [3]. If your terms are net 30 this figure should be 30 days or less.

▶ Cost of Goods Sold/Inventory

$$\frac{\text{Cost Of Goods Sold}}{\text{Inventory}}$$

Example

COGS/Inventory:

Cost of Sales	= 65% of sales	
	= $1,560,000 x 65% = $1,014,000	
Average Inventory	= $\frac{$225,450 + 253,500}{2}$ = $239,475	
COGS/Inventory	= $\frac{$1,014,000}{$239,475}$ = 4.2	

Try to use an average inventory figure rather than year-end or a similar unusual figure. The average inventory will give you a truer picture of how your business is actually doing over the course of the year.

▶ Days' Inventory

$$\frac{365}{\text{Cost of Goods Sold/Inventory}}$$

Example

Days' Inventory: $\frac{365}{4.2}$ = 87 days' inventory

This ratio is affected by your inventory cycle. It should average down to 45 days. This is a measure of how quickly you turn over your inventory. Higher is generally better, but an abnormally high or low ratio relative to industry figures is a danger sign. Either overtrading or the inability to maintain adequate inventories, a result of under-capitalization, causes too high a figure. This ratio doesn't take seasonal fluctuations into account. Cost of goods sold is used instead of net sales to eliminate imbalances caused by profit margins.

▶ Cost of Goods Sold/Payables

$$\frac{\text{Cost Of Goods Sold}}{\text{Trade Payables}}$$

Example

COGS/Payables: $\dfrac{\$530,250}{\$99,600} = 5.3$

Days' Payables: $\dfrac{365}{\text{COGS/Payables}}$ = 365 / 5.3 = 68.9 days

This measures annual turnover of trade payables (accounts payable). Higher values indicate a shorter time between purchase and payment. Generally lower numbers, down to the industry standard, indicate good performance. Below industry standards ("leaning on trade") can indicate liquidity problems. This ratio doesn't take seasonality into account.

▶ Sales/Working Capital

$$\frac{\text{Net Sales}}{\text{Net Working Capital}}$$

Example

Working Capital   = Current Assets - Current Liabilities
                   = 530,250 - 243,750 = 286,500

Sales/Working Capital: $\dfrac{\$1,560,000}{\$286,500} = 5.4$

Working capital is calculated by subtracting current liabilities from current assets. This ratio measures the margin of protection for current creditors and reflects the ability to finance current operations. It also measures how efficiently working capital is employed. A low value indicates inefficient use of working capital while a high ratio indicates a vulnerable position for creditors.

Coverage Ratios

Coverage ratios measure the company's ability to service debt, particularly bank debt. Bankers and other creditors look at these ratios very closely.

KEY INFO

▶ **EBIT/Interest**

$$\frac{\text{Earnings Before Interest} + \text{Taxes}}{\text{Annual Interest Expense}}$$

Example

EBIT/Interest: $\dfrac{\$148,050}{\$16,350} = 9.1$

In general, a higher ratio indicates a favorable capacity to take on additional debt.

Leverage Ratios

Leverage ratios measure exposure to risk and vulnerability to business downturns. The higher the leverage, the higher the risk and the higher the potential profits. Bankers examine these ratios closely, especially if the credit is not 100 percent secured by good collateral. Remember that bankers are by nature averse to risk.

KEY INFO

▶ **Fixed/Net Worth**

$$\frac{\text{Net Fixed Assets}}{\text{Tangible Net Worth}}$$

Example

Fixed/Net Worth: $\dfrac{\$534,750}{\$725,000} = 0.7$

This ratio measures the extent to which owner's equity has been invested in plant and equipment. For creditors, the lower the ratio the better. Note that the assets are net of depreciation and that "tangible net worth" washes intangibles (such as good will) off the books. Substantial leased assets may artificially and deceptively lower this ratio, which has been offered as a specious and potentially dangerous reason to lease plant and equipment rather than to buy it.

▶ Debt/Tangible Net Worth

$$\frac{\text{Total Liabilities}}{\text{Tangible Net Worth}}$$

Example

Debt/Tangible Net Worth: $\dfrac{\$340,000}{\$725,000} = 0.5$

Every banker looks at this measure of the relationship between debt and ownership. High ratios scare creditors, while low ratios may indicate excessive and unprofitable caution. Ask your banker what he or she would like this to be for a firm such as yours. If the answer doesn't make sense to you, explain why your ratio is whatever it is.

Operating Ratios

Operating ratios provide a measure of management performance. Comparing these ratios across time is one indicator of efficient management, subject to the usual "all things being equal" reservation.

▶ Profit Before Taxes/Net Worth

$$\frac{\text{Profit Before Taxes}}{\text{Tangible Net Worth}} \quad \text{x } 100$$

Example

Profit before taxes   = $131,700

PBT/Net Worth: $\dfrac{\$131,700}{\$725,000}$ x 100 = 18%

This is another ratio where very high or very low numbers indicate possible problems. A high ratio can mean that you are doing a great job. It could also mean that you are undercapitalized. A low value could be the result of overly conservative management of a well-capitalized company.

▶ Profit Before Taxes/Total Assets

$$\frac{\text{Profit Before Taxes}}{\text{Total Assets}} \quad \text{x } 100$$

Example

PBT/Total Assets: $\dfrac{\$131,700}{\$1,065,000}$ x 100 = 12.4%

This uses pre-tax profit to eliminate the vagaries of taxation. The higher the better, though it can be distorted by heavily depreciated assets, sizable intangible assets, or unusual income or expense items.

▶ Sales/Net Fixed Assets

$$\frac{\text{Net Sales}}{\text{Net Fixed Assets}}$$

Example

Sales/Fixed Assets: $\dfrac{\$1,560,000}{\$534,750} = 2.9$

This ratio measures the productive use of fixed assets. It also can be used, in conjunction with the next ratio and others, to estimate capital needs and how assets should be allocated in a startup.

▶ Sales/Total Assets

$$\frac{\text{Net Sales}}{\text{Total Assets}}$$

Example

Sales/Total Assets: $\dfrac{\$1,560,000}{\$1,065,000} = 1.5$

This ratio measures ability to generate sales in relation to total assets. Low assets or unusual sales patterns such as a startup will affect this.

▶ Sales/Number of Employees

$$\frac{\text{Total Sales}}{\text{Number of Employees}}$$

Example

Aardvark has 12 employees

Sales/Employee: $\dfrac{\$1,560,000}{12} = \$130,000$ per employee

This measures how well a business is using its employees, and is most often used as a comparative measure. A higher figure indicates either better equipment or better personnel management (or both).

18

Reading and Writing Footnotes

Footnotes are an important part of financial statements, whether you're reading them as an investor or as a concerned business owner. Financial statements without footnotes present only a piece of the picture and are seriously incomplete.

Footnotes flesh out the financials, provide supplemental information necessary for a proper understanding of the company, and supply context. If you have to have audited financials, an additional reason to take footnotes seriously is that you, the owner, are legally responsible for them. The auditor will look closely at them to make sure that you aren't fudging the numbers by concealing (for example) a major change in inventory valuation.

What should be footnoted? In the interest of transparency you want to provide information about any substantive changes or problems but you don't have to footnote everything. You couldn't—think how huge the financials would be if you did. This is a judgment you usually would make together with your accountant.

Some possible areas:

▶ **How you value inventory? Do you use LIFO or FIFO or some other method? Have you changed the valuation method from one to another? Why?**
▶ **How do you arrive at COGS?**
▶ **The nature and terms of long-term debts. What are the terms? When is payment due?**
▶ **What are your depreciation and amortization schedules? Do you use straight-line, accelerated, or a mix? Why did you choose them?**
▶ **Have you had to write down inventory, intangible assets, or accounts receivable (bad debts beyond the usual)? Why?**
▶ **If there are timing issues involved in recording revenues, be explicit.**

Perhaps the most important use of footnotes is that they document how you arrive at your forecasts and projections. Forecasts and projections are built on assumptions that are all too easy to forget. What assumptions will you make when forecasting sales? Just for starters, you'll make assumptions about the economy, competition, pricing, product mix, effectiveness of sales practices, marketing and advertising, continuity of suppliers, etc. The key is to ensure that you can rebuild your thoughts when it comes time to either explain your forecasts or recast them.

The same thing applies to the projected Profit & Loss and cash flow pro formas. Picture this scenario: You're sitting at your banker's desk. She's looking over your financing proposal that (you hope) demonstrates how a loan to your business is a safe investment for the bank and a way to make your business bigger and more stable. (Bankers like to see stable, profitable companies grow: Those companies will need more bank services, take out bigger credits, and make larger deposits. This is good for the bank's prospects.) She starts asking questions about specific parts of your projections. How did you arrive at this sales figure? Why do you think profits will go up so fast? Will you have to add several employees to do this or will the new equipment be enough to increase production?

That's where good footnotes (and appendices, which are a form of footnote for a financing proposal) can save the day. You want to project competence and credibility. If you can point out the assumptions underlying the numbers, footnotes, and appendices, your credibility will skyrocket.

Part Four

▼

Using the Financials to Manage Your Business

Forecasts, Budgets, Pro Formas, and More

19

Setting the Context: Part One of the Business Plan

A business plan is a roadmap—sketchy, maybe, and not 100 percent accurate (projections never are)—but a lot better than no map at all. You can keep up to six variables in your mind at any one time, but when you're running a small business, you have to keep tabs on a lot more than six variables. Your business plan helps you keep track of the variables and their effect on your business.

The description of business evolves into a mission statement, a brief sentence or two that eases decision-making and encourages focus on the right products, markets, and activities. A mission statement will help you identify your customers, provide a test of proposed actions, and save you from unnecessary errors.

The most basic planning decision involves understanding what business you're in—not an easy task. Since the rest of your planning efforts will be significantly affected by this early decision, it's smart to take it seriously.

You start writing your business plan with your ideas of what business you're really in, move to a careful consideration of what you sell, and then turn to a close scrutiny of your targeted markets. This is easier for an ongoing business than a startup/transition or fast-growth business but the same principles apply to them, as well. Once these are established, the remainder of the first part of your business plan is an explanation of how you'll achieve your goals: your facilities, personnel, and most important, your management.

Your business plan should answer these eight questions:

1. **What business are you really in?** Or: What is your "mission statement" or reason to be in business? This is a short (25 words or less) statement that defines your business

2. **What do you sell?** What do your customers think you sell? You may find that you don't know what you're selling, if what you sell is defined as what your customers buy. "My factories manufacture cosmetics," Charles Revson said, "We sell hope." He knew what he was selling.

3. **Who are your target markets?** The individuals who constitute your core market should be familiar to you. Not necessarily by name (unless your markets are extremely small), but rather by demographic descriptions (age, income, sex, educational level, lifestyles, etc.). Even if you sell to industrial or institutional markets, you sell to specific individuals. Who are they? What are they like? What are their titles? Who's involved in making the purchasing decision (influencers as well as gatekeepers)? Why, how, and when do they buy? This is vitally important knowledge. If you don't know it, drop everything and set about getting it. Now.

4. **How large are your markets?**

5. **What is (will be) your share of those markets?** Questions of market size and market share are slippery. A market that's defined too narrowly will be too small to permit growth or even survival—100 percent of a market of one is one customer. Markets too loosely defined ("everybody is a prospect! 4.6 billion people need this product!") can't be reached by any business, small or Fortune 500. Be realistic. Retail trade associations keep track of how many people are needed to support a store. If the trade experts say 20,000 people (popu-

lation of market area) are needed, and you are in a SMSA of 40,000 with only one competitor, fine. Seek out and use these numbers. The August issue of *Sales and Marketing Management* contains the Annual Survey of Buying Power and is an excellent source of demographic data.

Market share and demographics are heavily studied. A research librarian can help you tie Buying Power surveys to the most recent census information. Even better, Small Business Development Centers (an SBA program) and almost every business school can help you locate and apply this kind of information. What you want to do is make sure that your market is large enough to be profitable, small enough to be defended against competitors, and growing enough to satisfy your growth plans.

This is not simple, but it's an important part of financial management. Market share studies help you create realistic sales forecasts and budgets.

6. **Who are your competitors?** What share of the market do they enjoy? What is their pricing strategy? While price competition is usually the worst financial strategy, it's common. Keep an eye on the competition and you can benefit from imitating and improving on their successes and avoiding their errors. Just keeping competitor files on your five nearest competitors will put you in the competitive driver's seat.

7. **What resources can you allocate to projected sales growth?** Fast growth devours cash, capital, and credit, then gnaws at your basic running needs. The cash flow forecast helps you define the limits of growth. While energetic growth goals are fine to pursue, prudence demands that you be able to fund that growth. Otherwise you'll fall short—or worse yet, flat, as in broke.

8. **What personnel and management do you (will you) have available to implement your plans?**

There are many other factors to ponder in a business plan, but these eight questions are a good beginning. Your answers to them will help you set the goals embodied in your actual forecast.

T MORE

▶ Know Your Business

Frances Hesselbein, former head of the Girl Scouts of America, took over the Girl Scouts at a time when they had lost direction and were being pulled in many directions. While the Girl Scouts is a huge volunteer, nonprofit organization, it's no different in essence from any business. It had a structure, a fuzzy sense of what it was trying to do, and had to find a way to focus its efforts so it wouldn't outstrip its resources. This is exactly parallel to small business. The solution is not "work harder" or "sell more." It's more difficult: Know your business. What is its reason for existing? Hesselbein put the method and reason for working out a mission statement as clearly as anyone could: "We kept asking ourselves very simple questions. What is our business? Who is the customer? And what does the customer consider value? ... We really are here for one reason: to help a girl reach her highest potential. ... More than any one thing, that made the difference. Because when you are clear about your mission, corporate goals and operating objectives flow from it." Simple questions? You bet. Simple questions can be the hardest to answer.

Use your business plan to set and test goals. Your goals should be measurable and have time limits. For example, "Increase sales" is a poor goal (ill-defined, no time limits, not measurable) whereas "Increase sales 8 percent over last year by December" is clearly defined, time-limited, and measurable.

Your business goals should be realistic. Unrealistic goals are neither believable nor achievable. Unreachable goals breed frustration. Goals that are too easy generate boredom. The ideal goal is hard to reach but achievable, stretches abilities and skills, generates excitement, can be measured to note progress, has a reasonable time frame, and furthers the overall goals of the business. Business plans help business owners establish realistic business goals—then marshal their resources and create the organization to achieve them.

Why start a business that will only make you unhappy? People do it all the time because they set up a false dichotomy between personal goals and business goals. Your business should (ideally) reflect your personal values. Otherwise, it's almost impossible to maintain enthusiasm. You need to be enthusiastic to put in the hours and effort success requires.

Your personal goals provide a background for your plan. If personal and business goals are out of whack, the results will be disappointing no matter what the outcome. Some ideas: What do you want to accomplish before you retire? What if you had only five years to live—what are the most important goals for you to achieve? One year to go?

Some goals to consider setting: sales and profit; size of company by employees, assets, locations; product and service; high technology; civic responsibilities; altruistic or other non-economic goals.

Some other goal-setting questions: Will you have the stamina (both physical and mental) to achieve these goals? Will you have the patience to reach them? The motivation of the owner is a major factor in the success or failure of a small business.

Product/Service

Given the resources of a big business, the desires of the market can be considered before the product or service is defined. As a small business owner you lack that luxury. A plumber is not going to become an electrician because the demand for an electrician is greater in his or her market area. The background, experience, training, and capital of a small business owner are limiting factors. While you are encouraged to "take a marketing viewpoint" you probably won't radically change your business.

What will your customer really buy? What needs and wants do your products or service fill? This description will be used in the plan itself. This helps with the redefinition of your business, its markets, and goals. "What are you selling?" differs from "What are your products or services?" People buy solutions to their problems and satisfaction for their wants and needs. You sell more than a product or service. You meet needs, fill wants, and satisfy desires. Products or services are bought for emotional, not rational, reasons most of the time. Why buy one brand of toothpaste or car rather than another?

Benefits differ from features. Features are tangible qualities: size, weight, texture, finish, color. Solutions and satisfactions are the benefits your customers buy along with your products or services. You don't buy medical care—you buy health, pain relief, or reduction of anxiety. You don't buy a haircut—you buy sex appeal and image. And so on.

You have to give your market a reason to buy. Use product or service differentiation. This can be as simple as advertising convenience or price, or as complex as selling *Star Wars*. It has to be appropriate to your market, though, or it won't be effective.

How will you position your product or service? Some ideas: "New! Improved!", packaging, convenience, pricing, experience, skilled staff, advertising/promotion, delivery, open 24 hours.

Who are your target markets? This is the most basic piece of marketing information, one that comes up again and again. There's no product or service that everybody needs. You have to know who your customers (actual and potential) are, how many are available to you, and a host of other facts about them.

Why will people buy a product or service from you rather than from someone else? Note that this ties several pieces of the puzzle together. This is what marketing is all about—creating customers for your products or services. All benefit/feature analysis, all market differentiation and positioning are aimed at answering this question. Your answer starts with thorough product/service and target market knowledge.

Look at your products and services from the customers' point of view. Your challenge is to satisfy the customers and make a profit, which can't be done if you don't have a clear picture of what the customers really want.

What are you selling? Perfume is a small, prettily packaged bottle of liquid that smells nice. Maybe. But you really sell hope for success in love or status (not everyone can afford to buy French perfume at $1,200 an ounce) or the illusion that one is irresistible if properly scented. Advertising can be very persuasive, if somewhat silly.

The marketing section of your business plan is a plan within a plan. Investors are increasingly interested in how you answer: "Who will buy it? Why will they buy from you?"

Key points: The goal of a business plan is to gain greater sales and higher profits. Sales and profits stem from marketing—that is, creating customers who buy enough of your product or service often enough to provide you with acceptable profits. The marketing section of the business plan attempts to marshal the resources of the business to achieve those sales. You can argue this up one side and

▶ Product/Service

Look at your product or service as a bundle of features and benefits. And then stress the benefits, because that is what the public buys. Even industrial buyers are people with feelings and desires. The smart small business owner knows this and spends considerable time getting to know the benefits he or she is providing. This also helps you differentiate your goods from the competition's offerings. Finally, knowing which products are moneymakers and which are losers is of obvious importance if you seek to be profitable. (A minor quibble: you may want to invest in a product or service that is currently losing money for the sake of future gains.)

Features are inherent in the product or service while benefits are the "What's in it for me?" perceived by the customer. Features are used to convey benefits.

down the other: Does the marketing plan precede the business plan? Or does the business plan stem from the marketing plan? The truth is that they are interactive. The business plan has a wider focus and sets the conditions and restraints for marketing efforts. The marketing plan (which includes product/service analysis, competition, location, pricing, and other considerations, as well as knowledge about the specific current and prospective markets) drives the financial projections and goals, which in turn affect the business plan deeply. The section on marketing in the business plan is a condensed version of a more detailed marketing plan. Planning is a process, not a linear progression where you simply connect the dots and grind out the maximally effective business (and marketing) plan for your business, but an organic process.

There are steps to take, and a preferred order in which to take them. Each step is built on, presupposes, and impacts all the other steps, however, so in a sense you have to do everything at once. The result is a series of plans within plans. But there's another level of complexity to deal with. Business is done in a shifting economic and competitive climate. An effective plan anticipates these shifts, presents proactive responses, and seizes competitive advantage from them. All marketing is competitive. Business is competitive. Even nonprofit businesses (educational institutions) are competitive. They need to attract and retain their clients (students).

You have to know who your markets are and what they want. The only way to do this is to do some market research. You can't sit back in an armchair and by dint of sheer ratiocination come up with the answers. Plenty of people have learned this to their great cost. Markets are composed of people. The more tightly defined the market, the more you can get to know about your customers (actual and potential). Limit your target markets to fit your resources, make those folks happy, and then expand. Don't try it the other way, from the universal market down to the market you can realistically approach and impress.

There are plenty of other smart business owners looking to your customers for their growth. This continues the idea that nobody owns a market. There are only so many customers—profitable customers—out there. Pareto's Principle implies that 80 percent of your profits come from 20 percent of your customers. Those profit-producing customers are at risk.

Scouting the opposition is fair play. Major league managers and theatrical impresarios rely on scouting reports. The best way to find out where you stand on (for example) pricing, is to see what the other people are doing. Visit their store. Check prices. Ask questions. Are the clerks polite, well informed, helpful? Is the merchandise carefully chosen, clean, and attractive? Consider hiring a consultant to "shop" your own store.

Marketing strategy is best based on your strengths, the competitors' weaknesses, and the market's desires. Note how the business plan has addressed these. You have to know what your strengths are (product, location, personnel, financial, etc.). You have to know the competition inside out. Know the competition better than they know themselves. And you have to be attuned to the market. What do they want? What is their price tolerance? What level of quality and service do they demand? Then provide it.

Investors (including bankers) are interested in the quality of the management of your business. Investors need to know about the key employees and managers. These are the people who will put your plans into operation. What are their special talents? How will they be retained? How will you replace a key employee if he or she le

A succession plan is a must if you're seeking serious am
money. A succession plan lets your prospective investors kno
would happen should you be run over by a runaway truc
would take charge of your company until a successor is hired
would that process look like?

There are many examples of business plans at entreprene
and on the SBA Web site. Take a look at the varied formats an
the one that you think most closely resembles your company.
sure to cover the basics mentioned above.

20

Forecasting: Current and Anticipated Conditions

No business operates in a vacuum. External factors can batter even the most carefully managed business. Economic environments may change dramatically for the worse (or for better), new, well-heeled competitors might suddenly enter your market niche, laws and regulations affecting how you do business can cause you to lose sleep, new technologies might present you with great opportunities for growth.

Similarly, internal environments will affect you over the next few years. You might gain or lose an important employee, change your business model, develop new skills, find new markets, or develop new products.

You have to remain aware of the environments affecting your business. How can you best do this? Stay alert. Read the business press—*The Wall Street Journal, The New York Times*. Be active in your trade associations. Their editors act as distance warning systems, especially for technological shifts. Go to trade shows, talk with your competition, and other business owners. Your suppliers will often have a good notion of what's coming—they see orders rise or fall and they know what sectors are doing better or worse, and they want you to succeed. Make sure to ask your bankers and accountant what changes they foresee. They're in constant touch with other businesses in their advisory capacity. Ask your board of directors. The more input you get, the better your chances of making realistic forecasts.

Above all, don't blithely assume that business will chug along as usual. It won't. Your aim is to spot trouble coming before it hits and opportunities before they slip away.

Goals and Standards

Management and financial control compare actual performance to standards. These standards must be objective, measurable, and realistic. In baseball, you want your batters to reach or exceed .300, but don't plan on them batting .400 or better. Trying to attain the unreachable is fine for saints but downright demoralizing to the rest of the world.

Goals are easy to set, standards simple to choose. But to do it well is another matter. For a goal or standard to be believable, your employees (and you) have to feel that you have the resources and strategies to make that goal happen and have benchmarks along the way to keep your attention and enthusiasm up. If you think the goal is achievable, and it's not, no matter what you do or how hard you strive, the next set of goals will be less readily accepted.

Standards include goals, objectives, averages (including trade or industrial data), forecasts, and (re)statements of past performance. Put another way, goals and objectives are a special kind of standard. Averages function as a standard to measure performance against, though except in dire straits you wouldn't set them up as goals. "Be average!" is a poor rallying cry. Forecasts are based on your minimum goals or objectives, and become your budgets (a special form of goal) that establish the minimum acceptable level of performance. Historical performance is a fine indicator of historical performance. "Yes, that's what we did last year …," but unless you're inert or in a defensive mode, last year is merely a foundation for this year's goals. Last year's performance is normally used as the basis for a worst-case scenario, but in times of economic stress could be a difficult goal to achieve.

The business goals you set for the near future, based on the resources and markets available, find their expression in your forecasts. You have to ground your forecasts on a firmer foundation than wishful thinking, but if you think small you'll react small. Check your goals against both historical performance and industry/trade figures. These sets of figures provide a reality check. Your numbers shouldn't be copies of either, but adaptations of both. Look closely at significant differences and understand them, if only to forestall second-guessing by your banker.

Forecasts, especially sales forecasts, have a slippery quality even when you've carefully examined your business, its customers, and competition, economic climate, and all the other factors that affect your chances of reaching those goals and making your forecasts come true. This slipperiness is the main reason to dwell at length on how to create a worthwhile sales forecast. It's hard work. There are no valid shortcuts.

KEY INFO

▶ Forecasting/Goal Setting

Forecasting and goal setting are concurrent. The sequence is roughly this:

1. Set goals.
2. Express the goals in dollars or other numbers.
   P&L forecast (3-year)
   Cash flow forecast (3-year)
3. Project the balance sheet one year out to reflect P&L and cash flow changes.
4. Compare P&L and balance sheet forecasts to historical performance and trade figures.
5. Revise goals and forecasts as needed.

The criteria implicit throughout this process are loose: "makes good sense for my business," "realistic goals for my business under given conditions," and "goals worth committing ourselves to achieving." Your understanding and experience, aided by research, afford the best reality check on the goals and forecasts, and that grounding in reality is a key element in preparing useful goals and forecasts.

Goal Setting

Even before setting the initial numbers in your sales and expense forecasts, review your goals. These come in two flavors: your personal
goals, which are primary, and your goals for your business over the
next few years. Your business goals are subordinate to your personal
goals, or should be, even though the two sets are most likely inter-
twined. Your business life should support your personal life. That is,
if you want to retire in five years to travel, or sell your business in two
years to pursue another activity, your goals for the business would be
different than if you plan to grow the business indefinitely because it's
so much fun to do so. The broad, often subjective personal goals provide subtle limits on business plans, which have to be specific.

Your business is a startup or transitional business, an ongoing business, or a fast-growth business. Which stage your business is in makes
a significant difference to your forecasts. The ordinary ongoing business,
which has enough momentum going for it to make sudden changes unlikely, is the simplest to forecast. The majority of businesses fit this mold.

Companies in a startup or other transition phase pose a particular problem: they will almost always veer from their initial goals.
"Transitional" companies come in several guises. Unlike the startup
business, a transitional business has a history to help guide it and
define goals. But during the transitional period (shift of ownership
or management, major changes in the marketplace or technology or
economy), it's more like a startup than an ongoing business. Their
goals tend to be fluid, similar businesses are hard to locate because
most trade and industry data is based on the average performance,
and—the deciding factor—historical performance is no longer pertinent. Because the business must in some critical sense be reestab-
lished, with completely or substantively new goals and forecasts, treat
a transitional company as if it were a startup. This is especially important when dealing with a turnaround situation, where the business is
either dead in the water or close to it.

Fast-growth companies are high-risk companies, driven by their
markets, which makes goal-setting beyond "meet the demand" and
"don't run out of cash" extremely difficult. The most important goal
is liquidity, since fast growth devours cash at a frightening pace. This
does not mean that you needn't set goals and make forecasts if you
were riding a fast-growth business. You should, but be prepared to

shift gears and rethink both goals and forecasts more frequently than in the other stages. Startup, transitional, and ongoing businesses will normally function well with goals and plans revised no more often than every six months (or a year, if the forecasts hold true). Fast-growth businesses need to rethink their numbers as often as monthly and at all times have a contingency plan available to meet the threat of running into the wall and becoming illiquid.

Before proceeding to the forecasts, speak with your salespeople (sales manager, marketing manager, line salespeople) to get their advice on what sales levels can reasonably be set. In a very small business, everyone will have ideas to offer.

Use marketing research to set sales goals (top down) and sales requirements to cover costs and profits (bottom up). Your sales force will help you determine whether the goals are reasonable.

SWOT Analysis

A SWOT analysis can be helpful to any business interested in setting meaningful goals. SWOT stands for Strengths, Weaknesses, Opportunities, and Threats.

Start a SWOT analysis by poring over the internal strengths and weaknesses of the business. You have some control over these. Your employees know what is working well and what isn't. Your aim here is to find the most important strengths (to build on) and weaknesses (so you can correct them).

Next turn to analysis of the external environment. What are the opportunities and threats that your business faces? Sales personnel know the customers better than the engineering department, while the engineers will understand the changing technologies better than the lawyers, who understand the legal and political environments better than you do. And so on. Nobody is a universal business genius. Those who appear to be geniuses (for example, Bill Gates of Microsoft, Warren Buffett of Berkshire Hathaway) are super collectors of information from a variety of experts, both within their firms and without. That skill helps them make the right decisions about the most important matters.

SWOT structures your information concisely enough to make decisions on that compiled information.

After the SWOT has been completed, the next step is to decide what the most important strengths and opportunities, weaknesses and threats are. The general rule is to concentrate your strengths on the greatest opportunities, while shoring up weak areas and avoiding threats. This has to be done carefully: It's where you choose where to place your bets. What are the right things to do? The goals and their derivative short-term objectives provide the best ways to capitalize on those strengths and opportunities.

This is as strategic as you can get. The importance of focus cannot be overstated. Limit your efforts over the next twelve months to dealing with the two or three most promising strengths and opportunities and the two or three most dangerous threats or weaknesses. Don't try to deal with more. In fact, dealing with one or two will keep you busy.

These are examples of the kinds of things other businesses look at when doing their SWOT analyses. Customize it to suit your needs.

 TABLE

▶ Internal Analysis:
Strengths and Weaknesses

Factor	Strengths	Weaknesses
Quality		
Customer Service		
Financial Resources		
Financial Management		
Operations		
Production		
Staff		
Training		
Management		
Communication		

▶ External Analysis:
Opportunities and Threats

Factor	Opportunities	Threats
Current Customers		
Prospects		
Competition		
Technology		
Political Climate		
Government & Regulatory Bodies		
Legal		
Economic Environment		

21

Sales and Expense Forecasting

Methods of forecasting sales range from sheer guesswork on the one hand to pseudo-statistical analysis on the other. For small business owners, the preferred method is the three-way approach illustrated on page 121 below. Its strength is that it looks at the firm's sales from a number of viewpoints. Each chunk is a separate scenario, with its own assumptions and justification. The three totals (Worst, Best, Most Likely) summarize those assumptions and provide a way to explain how the totals were determined. Since each scenario gives another chance to look at how the business operates in its environments, it's an invaluable learning tool.

Note that sales projections aren't simple guesses or exercises in wishful thinking. They're constructs, built up product line by product line, or sales area by sales area, or market by market (or whatever other chunks are used to break sales down into manageable bites.) Past performance helps set a floor for future sales. Trade figures help for startups, as well as providing guidelines for going concerns. But since they are aggregate figures, use them only to check the reasonableness of the sales projections, not as a starting point. If the sales projections are in the ballpark, so will the goals that use them as a base.

Establishing a sales forecast is the first step in putting your goals into numbers. Sales drive every business, whether brand new, in transition, or just chugging along. They affect all expenses, if only in a negative way (if you have no sales, how do you pay the bills?). Some expenses are fixed within the limits of a certain sales range, while others vary directly with sales, which is another reason to start with sales forecasting.

All forecasts are ultimately based on assumptions and hunches, a meld of information and experience, and as such, won't be 100 percent accurate. That's fine. One hundred percent accuracy is a chimerical goal, unattainable and in many cases an excuse for inaction. A 95 percent accuracy level would be outstanding. You should be happy to hit 80 percent. Start with your sales goals.

The problem now shifts to the composition of those sales and the likelihood of attaining them. Both the P&L and cash flow projections start with sales. The following method is effective for short-term (up to one year) forecasts. Two- or three-year goals are less accurate but provide some direction for your business, and as you will be revising your forecasts at least annually, tend to self-correct. If you need to forecast beyond three years, you'll be in the realm of pure guesswork. Even forecasting beyond six months or one year is fraught with pitfalls. The distant numbers you generate have a specious aura of authority ("Let's see: five years' compounded annual growth rate of 30 percent …") that reality laughs at. This is one place where computerized spreadsheets can lead anyone astray.

As you follow the sales forecasting process, make notes. The assumptions you base your numbers on are filtered by your experience, and should be checked against your own industry and historical figures as part of the full forecasting process. If you forget to document your assumptions as you go along, it's unlikely that you'll remember what those assumptions were several weeks or months later. Scrutinizing your assumptions in order to correct and improve them is an integral part of managing by the numbers that is easily overlooked.

Method 1

Some owners and managers like to start with profit goals, following the excellent idea that "Profit is a fixed expense." If your business traditionally achieves 8 percent pre-tax profit on sales, then it's a simple calculation to determine the sales levels you need to attain a projected dollar profit.

▶ Determining Sales From Profit Goals

Sales needed: X
Profit (pre-tax) as % of Sales: 8%
Projected profit (goal): $150,000

X = $150,000/8% = $1,875,000

This method is not recommended for either startup/transitional or fast-growth businesses. If you don't have a consistent profitability picture (these kinds of businesses don't by definition), any profitability percentage is as good as any other. For an ongoing business, it can be a helpful check on the sales figures derived by Method 2 below.

To avoid wrestling with a lump sales figure ($1,875,000 for the desired profit example), break the gross figure into its component parts. Product lines are one way to do this. Another useful method is to divide sales by market area: so much to industrial, so much to institutional, so much to individual; or by sales method: direct sales, retail sales.

Method 2

Determine, for each product line or market segment, the *most likely* annual sales by figuring the worst case, the best case, and then the most likely case. The resulting total sales figure is a construct that you can use with fair confidence; it's not a grab at thin air. There are several ways to dice your onions. Begin with a look at last year's sales, broken down by market segment. Or break it down by product line. This is a matter of choice.

This past year Aardvark's sales broke down as follows:

Segment	
Safety Equipment	$375,000
Overstock & Special	$130,000
Recreational Marine	$535,000
Traditional Rigging	$285,000
Outdoors/Camping	$235,000
Total Sales	**$1,560,000**

The procedure is this: for each product line or market segment or whatever chunks you choose to use, list the worst case sales estimate. This is what you can see happening if everything goes wrong. The economy sours, your customers find other suppliers, new competitors enter the fray, price wars break out, and your sales force defects. This highly unlikely scenario is useful for a couple of reasons. First, it will later be the basis for your contingency plan, which is handy in case your banker desires to see it. Second, by looking at what might go wrong on an incremental basis you can't help but look ahead—and thus prevent or avoid many deadfalls.

Aardvark's owner decided that the worst case scenario would be 90 percent of last year's sales. The five product lines have been slowly growing, but who knows?

Segment	Worst Case	Most Likely	Best Case
Safety	$337,500		
Overstock	$117,000		
Recreational Marine	$481,500		
Traditional Rigging	$256,500		
Outdoors/Camping	$211,500		
Total Sales	**$1,404,000**		

Ordinarily, if these product lines are or "feel" stable and if you have no intimation of radical change—and if you don't plan any unusual activities yourself—you can expect to come close to last year's sales figures as a worst case scenario. "Close" means in the 90 percent range. Since Aardvark sold $1,560,000 last year, this year they'd be distressed and surprised to do worse than $1,404,000 (90 percent).

The process continues. Using historical figures, tempered by experience and the judgment of the sales force, Aardvark looked at each product line in turn. The net result: worst case sales total of $1,404,000.

Now comes the fun part. What does Aardvark (realistically) think their best case would be? The same kind of analysis goes on. New products are well received, old products continue to chip in sales, and new opportunities come up. This is not a pie in the sky exercise, but a carefully thought-out "what if ..." scenario. Aardvark doesn't expect a new product to sell 100,000 units in its first year. They would like it, but the chances are so remote that they don't let it infect the forecasting process. Nor do they assume that there is a pent-up demand for their products in declining markets. Each best-case figure represents a mini scenario. The numbers are reasoned judgments, estimates based on their knowledge of and experience with their products and markets.

Key point: Your forecasts depend on your knowledge of your products and your markets. Not on trade averages, not on wishful thinking, not on fantasy or magic. If your forecasts are to be useful, they must represent the quantification of your conclusions drawn from your experience, research, hunches, and goals. You need research (including input from employees and other persons) and facts (such as trade data) to test your forecasts. But your forecasts ultimately embody your ideas.

To continue: Keep notes to remind you of how you arrived at your figures. In a simplified version:

▶ Aardvark Inc. Forecasting

Segment	Worst Case	Most Likely	Best Case
Safety	$337,500		$450,000
Overstock	$117,000		$175,000
Recreational Marine	$481,500		$700,000
Traditional Rigging	$256,500		$410,000
Outdoors/Camping	$211,500		$310,000

Notes:
- ▶ Safety: We can increase this line with more aggressive marketing and an influx of new products. Sales of new products should increase by around $100,000.
- ▶ Overstocks and special items can increase if we add them to our Web site in a more prominent way. People love bargains.

▶ Recreational marine will resume being a growth market as the economy eases. Last year's sales were flat because of the severe recession and the drop in the stock market. Recreational marine products are optional and many boaters were reluctant to spend cash on their hobby.

▶ Traditional rigging increased a little last year. Maybe owners of old classics aren't willing to let their boats deteriorate? This product line has already shown signs of strong growth, up 20 percent in the last quarter.

▶ Outdoors/camping will grow if we pursue it. We've let it trot gently along with almost no marketing. An increase on the order of $100,000 isn't far from out of the question if we (a) increase marketing and advertising for this segment, and (b) find a better way to train sales staff to promote it as an add-on, since many of our customers are campers, as well as boaters.

Note that in this part of the forecasting process Aardvark is already examining strategies to help reach the goals in the best case scenarios. They always plan for growth (not that they always get it).

In the worst case scenario you look at problems you might face. In the best case you're more interested in opportunities and ways to increase sales. In the final step, the most likely scenario, pull these ideas together to better understand your opportunities and form strategies to take advantage of them. The most likely scenario shapes the structure and content of the operating budgets, the P&L, and cash flow pro formas that become key company-wide standards. It also provides a third run through of your forecast.

Three forecast revisions may look like overkill but it's not an onerous chore. The benefits are huge: each new run through gives you another chance to test assumptions and express ideas. Forecasting sales' greatest benefits come from this focused attention.

Segment	Worst Case	Most Likely	Best Case
Safety	$337,500	$400,000	$450,000
Overstock	$117,000	$145,000	$175,000
Recreational Marine	$481,500	$625,000	$700,000

Traditional Rigging	$256,500	$350,000	$410,000
Outdoors/Camping	$211,500	$275,000	$310,000
Total Sales	**$1,404,000**	**$1,795,000**	**$2,045,000**

The largest potential increases deserve the most attention. To get the best return on your efforts, focus on only a few of your product lines or markets. This does not mean that you should neglect large pieces of your business. It means you should set priorities, a baffling command that makes consultants and bankers sound as if they knew what they were talking about.

Since Aardvark has strong reasons to expect significant increases in recreational marine and traditional rigging, the most likely figures are skewed toward best case. Modest increases are expected elsewhere (remember: assume worst case sales no worse than 90 percent of last year's), with the mild exception of the overstock products.

Once again, each line is a scenario. The most likely case for each market is based on Aardvark's knowledge of its products and markets, continuously updated. It doesn't take a simple average of worst case and best case. To do so would waste the benefits of this process.

If you're more comfortable with a mathematical approach, you could assign weights (probabilities) to the worst and best cases.

For example:

Segment	Worst Case	Most Likely	Best Case
Safety	$337,500 (10%)		$450,000 (60%)

Suppose there's a slim (10 percent) chance of the worst case occurring, and an excellent chance (60 percent) of the best case coming to pass. The weighted average (most likely) becomes:

$$\frac{(1 \times 337{,}500) + (6 \times 450{,}000)}{7} = \sim 434{,}000$$

Similar assignments of probabilities produce other weighted averages. Some people swear by this technique. The three-case informal technique, if you keep notes on your assumptions as you go along, is better for most small business owners. Over several years (or economic cycles) you'll learn to spot indicators that will enhance your forecasting ability. This can't be done if you rely on your computer to spit out predictions based on the past and trade data modulated by some probability factor.

Perhaps more important from a psychological viewpoint, you only value forecasts you own by dint of effort and thought. Sure, you can plot points and design curves to fit, or use other techniques, but you miss the benefits that come from scrutinizing a wide variety of scenarios.

TABLE

▶ Sample Forecasting Scenarios

Segment	Worst Case	Most Likely	Best Case
...			

Or:

Profit Centers	Worst Case	Most Likely	Best Case
...			

Or:

Sales Territories	Worst Case	Most Likely	Best Case
Bert (NE)			
Brad (SE)			
Sonya (Central)			
Willie (West Coast)			
...			

Or:

Product Lines	Worst Case	Most Likely	Best Case
Boats			
Motors			
Materials & Supplies			
Services			
...			

Some of the questions to ask (of each profit center) are:

1. **What is the potential for one year? For Three or five years out?**
2. **How easily can we make this grow?**
3. **What are the margins? Are they increasing, decreasing, or flat?**
4. **How much will it cost (dollars, people) to achieve this growth? Can we afford it?**
5. **Are the trends up or down?**

As a rule of thumb: Don't try to break out more than six or eight product lines, markets, divisions, or other components. If you do, you lose sight of the forest in a welter of trees. For most businesses, four or five are sufficient.

Special Cases: Startup/Transition, Fast Growth

Startups have particularly difficult sales forecasting problems—difficult but not insoluble. With no prior sales experience for the business, other guidelines are needed.

The danger is ignoring the first law of business physics: a business at rest tends to remain at rest. Trade and industry figures are derived from the performance of ongoing businesses. This skews the figures toward a different shape. New businesses tend to have sales lower than their expenses might justify, and all too often less capital than they really need to get sales levels up to a profitable level.

What's the solution?

The same three-column approach works. To be conservative, figure the best case first, basing it on the top performers' performance (top quartile of Robert Morris Associates or Financial Research Associates trade ratios.). At best you'll be able to get to this level in the first year. You presumably think you can, otherwise, why go into business? But it's unlikely that you'll do better.

1. **Look at the Sales-to-Net Worth ratio.** This enables you to estimate the level of sales you could attain given the capital invested in the business. The amount of capital invested or borrowed helps determine the sales level you can reach. This becomes crucial for growing businesses, as their receivables tend to outstrip their capital base. Beyond a certain point, lenders won't provide capital for fast growth and will require more invested capital. This leverage problem is particularly irksome for rapidly growing businesses. While net worth and invested capital aren't always the same, they are at startup, since there are no retained earnings to play with. If the top quartile has a Sales/Net Worth ratio of 15 and you have $50,000 invested capital, sales in the $750,000 range, while improbable, are possible. The worst case and most likely case are then roughed in (as before: your judgment

and experience play their role here), and you end up with an aggregated sales figure. Break this out as a reality check.

2. **Once you've established the most likely range, take the figures to your banker, financial advisor, or other trusted expert.** Be prepared to have your figures challenged because your natural, laudable, and agreeable optimism will have clouded your judgment. Remember: the payoff is in the performance, not in the projections. You can try to prove them wrong—but plan pessimistically. It pays off.

3. **Now: recast your forecasts.** Time spent here pays you back in numerous ways. You'll develop more realistic sales forecasts, you'll go through a minimum of six iterations, and in so doing, develop greater understanding of your proposed business.

Key Point: Your forecasts become the working model of your business, once you add the expenses and debt loads. The P&L and cash flow are designed to provide a working model of your business. A reasonableness criterion is implicitly involved here: are these numbers reasonable, given the economic and competitive situation you find yourself in?

Transitional businesses, including turnarounds and ownership changes, face a slightly different set of problems. There's an operating history to serve as a worst case guide, but there's some question of how applicable that history is. If the business is in a slide, a perverse momentum develops. You have to first halt the slide, and then reverse the momentum. This is always harder and takes longer than you expect. Most ownership changes involve a degree of lost momentum, if only because a few employees are going to be distracted or a few key customers might defect.

1. **All transitional businesses need a completely new business plan.** A key part of this plan is a fresh look at both products/ services and markets. Unlike an ongoing business that has a wide range of ways to forecast its sales, transitional businesses must reexamine both sides of the product/market mix.

2. **Do two sales forecasts.** One sales forecast should be by product line, a second by major market segments. This forces at-

tention on your customers, which is exactly where it should be. The same worst case/best case process is used as before.

Year Before Last	Last Year	Current Year (annualized)	Worst Case
$300,000	$270,000	$180,000 for 9 months, $240,000 if annualized	$144,000

An example of a serious decline: Extrapolating from nine-months' performance annualizes current year's performance. If the actual figures are:

80,000 IQ

60,000 IIQ

40,000 IIIQ

your annualization would be considerably lower. If IVQ is the strongest in most years, the annualization might be higher. The point is to look at how the numbers are generated before leaping to conclusions. While an ordinary going business can use 90 percent of previous year (excepting unusual cases, such as banks), use a lower multiplier. How low depends on the severity of the transition. A turnaround might look at a 40 percent or 50 percent factor, while an ownership change, well-orchestrated and smooth, could look at 80 percent to 90 percent. It will vary. There's no mechanical way to grind out these percentages. Too much judgment is involved.

3. **Historic momentum is more powerful than trade averages in figuring the near-term forecast, especially when tempered by your knowledge of current economic and market conditions.** Once again, test your forecasts against your banker, financial advisor, or other expert. If you're new to this line of business, or are trying to effect a traumatic change in direction of one you know well, get all the help you can. Your banker will probably haul out trade data, which is helpful if somewhat beside the point. However, it forces yet another look at your assumptions, and is valuable for that reason.

Fast Growth

If you're the fortunate owner of a fast-growth business, you are probably too busy to be reading this, let alone follow the suggestions, but just in case...

1. **You need two forecasts, one assuming the fast growth will continue, the other assuming that it will not.**

	Slow Growth			Fast Growth		
	Worst	Most Likely	Best	Worst	Most Likely	Best
A.						
B.						
C.						
D.						
E.						
Total						

   You need both of these forecasts to satisfy your creditors, vendors, bankers, and your own informational needs. The first helps you get a handle on your cash and capital needs. The second provides a fallback plan, a lowered set of cash and capital needs. Fast growth won't last forever, and if you continue to grow, you'll be hiring experts to help with a different level of financial management and control well beyond the scope of this book.

2. **You'll also have to revise your forecast more frequently than either a startup/transitional or ongoing business.** Where they would revise no more often than every six months, if not just once a year, fast growth demands ongoing revisions to the sales forecast, as the stakes are higher and greater importance attaches to quickly detecting changes in the sales pattern and making corrections to the cash flow projection. If you don't demand this of yourself, your bankers will. Why? High growth equals high risk. Rapidly growing markets can get swamped when large companies leap in.

3. **Neither history nor trade figures are much help in the continued fast-growth scenario.** Trade figures are of value in the fallback scenario, as conditions return to a normal state. You may be able to find analogous businesses, which, while not

in the precisely same industry, are close by reason of product, market, or structure. Fast-changing examples abound: search engines, for example. First there was Archie, then Excite, Galaxy, Yahoo!, Lycos, Alta Vista, AskJeeves, and (drum roll) Google and Bing. There may be no trade data worth using. Fast-growth businesses tend to be found in fast-growth sectors of the economy. Even in retailing, a new concept (such as Toys R Us) carves a new industry niche. Not until after the fast-growth years are over will you find really helpful trade data developed.

Forecasting Sales and Planning Profits

Your sales forecast is almost finished, but not quite. Two important operations have to be performed on it: First you have to extrapolate or extend it to three years (five, if your financial sources insist). Second, you have to take the annual figures and break them down by month for the first year, and quarterly for years two through five.

Forecasting more than a year is most useful as a goal-setting exercise. Since you should prepare sales forecasts at least once a year, preferably more often, any egregious errors will be corrected over time. If your long-term plans call for expansion, these forecasts help you understand your capital needs as well as the kind of financing most apt to be secured.

Long-range sales forecasting in a small business is a chancy affair at best. You can extrapolate current trends: If you have enjoyed 15 percent annual sales growth and anticipate continued growth, extrapolation works. You can use linear regression analysis on changes in annual growth rates, or consult chicken entrails, or consult an economist. You're still going to be dealing with extrapolated guesses guided by your experience. Long-range forecasts don't have to be highly accurate, which is just as well. They seldom are accurate.

Why forecast two to five years out, then? It helps to set out goals, and to see what your business would look like if the sales forecasts were met. As in earlier forecasts, the greatest value in the forecasting process is the questions you raise and answer. As for any direct operational value of these long-range forecasts (beyond helping you investigate various scenarios), there's little. They help you arrange financing. Bankers love forecasts. They guide you in the paths of fiscal prudence. They help you spot opportunities before your competitors do. Just thinking in long time frames provides a measure of directional stability: We want these sales levels in three years. What do we have to do between now and then to reach that goal? The one-year budgets provide the operational control. The long budgets establish a framework for planning.

1. **What are your plans?** For example, if you will open other stores, add other product lines, begin to sell in new or foreign markets, your sales should increase. How much, will of course depend, but you have some idea of the goals.
2. **What are industry trends?** No boom lasts forever. No bust does either.
3. **What are the economic trends in your markets and in the more general economy?** Reading general business papers (*The Wall Street Journal* or the major city dailies), magazines (*Business Week, Forbes,* and so on), and books helps. Keeping alert pays off, and helps you understand the general context in which your business play unfolds.

   Don't make the optimistic error of thinking you can spot the turns specifically, and base plans on that assumption. You can spot the turns in a general sense, and be prepared to take advantage of them, but it's risky to count on a wisdom nobody else has ever maintained. Even the experts are occasionally mistaken.
4. **What competitive, technological, or other factors will be likely during the forecast period?**

Long-term forecasting for small businesses is seldom very accurate, but it is more to your advantage to try it, keeping in mind that you'll have plenty of chances to revise your forecast.

22

The Pro Forma
P&L

Turning Sales Forecasts Into
Projected Profit & Loss Statements

Sales forecasts are useful in and of themselves, but their most important use is as the basis for the projected profit & loss (P&L) and cash flow. These two projections lead directly to changes in the balance sheet, which can also be treated as a projection. If you're going to use your projections to substantiate a financing proposal, a projected balance sheet is often required. To be on the safe side, have your accountant check your figures. Nothing deflates a proposal quite as thoroughly as projections that don't fit together.

The process now becomes relatively mechanical. Your sales forecast is the key. Sales affect all of the expense items on the P&L, and that ripples over into the cash flow.

Sales forecast ⟶

          P&L projection ⟶

                   Cash flow pro forma

Keep notes as you prepare your projections. You'll need a record of how or why you chose this figure or that one. As experience corrects your forecasts, it helps to review what gave rise to the disparities between projected and actual performance. There will be some totally unexpected forces that blow projections apart. More often the cause will be an accumulation of small changes, and as you become more experienced and knowledgeable, fewer of these will surprise you. Your annotated projections are much stronger guides than the bare numbers alone could be.

Projections give you a framework for making decisions and measuring progress. They provide an important preview of changes you plan to make. They help you establish budgets, but they aren't meant to be a straitjacket.

Some points to keep in mind as you project your P&L:

1. **Documentation is the hardest part of the projected P&L.** The projected P&L *must* be well documented. Each item that appears is there because you have made some assumptions. If you can recapture that assumption six months down the road, when sales are off or an expense has exploded on you, you'll be able to improve future projections by avoiding the mistake implicit in the flawed assumption. Why do you expect a change in some item? Why do you expect business as usual?

2. **Note that profits don't guarantee survival.** You can make a profit and run out of cash. *Illiquidity*—the inability to meet current liabilities—is a common problem in growing businesses. Increased sales become increased receivables that have to be financed. Inventory has to be larger. Personnel have to be added. New, larger facilities are needed. New equipment is needed. All of these are cash drains, so the next step is (frequently) new debt, which in turn drains more cash. The cure is more invested capital.

3. **The longer the time span the less accurate the projection.** Some banks and other capital sources like to see a five-year projection. Many small business experts say that's absurd. A one- to three-year projection is more than enough to make a credit judgment. Once you go beyond thirty-six months, a projection is guesswork. (Even that lengthy a period is dubious.) A 12-month projection, broken down by months, is a

valuable guide to management. That level of detail doesn't help too much beyond the first year, but annual (or semi-annual) updates should be made.

4. **Be realistic.** Both optimism and pessimism are traps. Too much optimism leads to over-investment, while excessive conservatism (pessimism) pinches the company's prospects.

Step 1

Look at last year's sales to see if there are any patterns. Aardvark's monthly sales broke out as follows:

2011 Totals By Month	Jan	Feb	Mar	Total
Safety	$31,400	$18,750	$18,750	$68,900
Overstock	85,000	10,000	2,000	97,000
Recreational Marine	42,800	26,750	26,750	96,300
Traditional Rigging	22,800	14,250	14,250	51,300
Outdoors/Camping	18,800	11,750	11,750	42,300
Monthly Total	**$200,800**	**$81,500**	**$73,500**	**$355,800**
Cumulative Monthly Total	**$200,800**	**$282,300**	**$355,800**	

Notice that the sales have been broken down by category as in the sales forecast. This facilitates analysis of each product line. January is artificially large because of an annual post-Christmas overstock sale. Other lines are low in January, February, and March as boaters are waiting for spring.

Here are Aardvark's sales by quarter. This has been a stable pattern for years, with Q2 and Q3 being the most active months as boaters and campers (an overlapping market to some degree) get to boat and camp. Remember that extra financial factors affect forecasts.

2011 Totals By Quarter	1st	2nd	3rd	4th	Total
Safety	$68,900	$120,000	$100,000	$87,500	$376,400
Overstock	97,000	3,000	3,000	27,000	130,000
Recreational Marine	96,300	200,000	145,700	93,000	535,000
Traditional Rigging	51,300	85,000	95,000	55,000	286,300
Outdoors/Camping	42,300	75,000	75,000	40,000	232,300
Total	**$355,800**	**$483,000**	**$418,700**	**$302,500**	**$1,560,000**
% Annual sales	**23%**	**31%**	**27%**	**19%**	**100%**

Step 2

Project the 2012 sales, using 2011 sales as a template.

2012 Projected Sales	
Safety	$400,000
Overstock	$145,000
Recreational Marine	$625,000
Traditional Rigging	$350,000
Outdoors/Camping	$275,000
Total	**$1,795,000**

Now spread the sales:

2012 Totals By Month	Jan	Feb	Mar	Total
Safety	$36,110	$21,563	$21,563	$79,235
Overstock	97,750	11,500	2,300	111,550
Recreational Marine	49,220	30,763	30,763	110,745
Traditional Rigging	26,220	16,388	16,388	58,995
Outdoors/Camping	21,620	13,513	13,513	48,645
Monthly Total	**$230,920**	**$93,725**	**$84,525**	**$409,170**
Cumulative Monthly Total	**$230,920**	**$324,645**	**$409,170**	

Once again to spare you too many numbers:

2012 Totals By Quarter	1st	2nd	3rd	4th	Total
Safety	$79,235	$138,000	$115,000	$100,625	$432,860
Overstock	111,550	3,450	3,450	31,050	149,500
Recreational Marine	110,745	230,000	167,555	106,950	615,250
Traditional Rigging	58,995	97,750	109,250	63,250	329,245
Outdoors/Camping	48,645	86,250	86,250	46,000	267,145
Total	**$409,170**	**$555,450**	**$481,505**	**$347,875**	**$1,794,000**
% Annual Sales	**23%**	**31%**	**27%**	**19%**	

Step 3

Look closely at COGS. Aardvark's COGS has been steady at 65 percent of net sales. This was a major target area for improvement—65 percent is a bit over trade averages of 60 percent of net sales. Aardvark's management wanted to improve the gross margin and thus improve the bottom line, and took steps to do this by improving their inventory purchasing procedures. They feel confident that they can have COGS at or below trade averages next year.

Retailers like Aardvark find that the price paid for products is particularly crucial. It's usually the greatest area of expenditure. Any business can benefit from an analysis of COGS, as it can highlight ways to improve efficiency and cut expenditures.

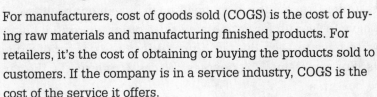

▶ Defining COGS

For manufacturers, cost of goods sold (COGS) is the cost of buying raw materials and manufacturing finished products. For retailers, it's the cost of obtaining or buying the products sold to customers. If the company is in a service industry, COGS is the cost of the service it offers.

COGS is closely related to inventory—which is treated as potential revenue in relation to tax—so it's also essential information for a company's profit and loss account (income tax return).

A 5 percent improvement would add more than $50,000 to Aardvark's net profit. A key assumption for the projection: Aardvark's buying procedures will improve enough in the first quarter to reach the desired 60 percent objective.

▶ Computing COGS

Cost Of Goods Sold	= Beginning Merchandise Inventory
	+ Net Purchases of Merchandise
	− Ending Merchandise Inventory

Example:

Aardvark's beginning Merchandise Inventory	=	$225,450
Net Purchases of Merchandise	=	$1,042,100
Ending Merchandise Inventory	=	$253,500
COGS = 225,400 + 1,042,100 − 253,500	**=**	**$1,014,000**

Step 4

Variable expenses go up and down as sales go up and down, and are calculated as a percent of anticipated sales. These will figure prominently in breakeven analysis. *Variable costs* are those that respond directly and proportionately to changes in activity level or volume, such as raw materials, hourly production wages, sales commissions, inventory, packaging supplies, and shipping costs.

Other operating expenses are fixed, coming up the same each time. Fixed expenses (the "nut") crop up whether you have sales or not. These payments include rent, utilities, lease payments, insurance, and basic running costs of your business. Keeping fixed costs under firm control is an ongoing management problem, since you have to gear up for anticipated sales or lose potential business, but also have to keep the nut down or face the danger of runaway costs. For most small businesses, Wages & Salaries is the largest fixed cost item.

A few expenses are mixed, with elements of both fixed and variable. Telephones and postage, and some advertising and marketing costs have this complexion.

The convention for fixed expenses is that they are spread evenly across the year. Unless you have a good reason (which you would annotate), take the total annual expense and divide by 12. This applies to insurance, legal, and accounting expenses, even if you pay them quarterly or annually. Your accountant can help you set up these projected expenses.

Fixed expenses are fixed only within limits. As your business grows, you will need more employees, more space, more equipment and so forth, which in turn, will drive up fixed expenses. Unfortunately, trimming fixed expenses in periods of slow sales is more difficult than adding fixed expenses in good times. The general rule of thumb is never to increase these fixed expenses until you are forced to. Opportunity costs won't put you out of business, but fixed expenses might.

The figures in your projected P&L will be your operating standards, so it behooves you to proceed carefully. As a guideline, use your most recent P&L, even if it is last year's. You can always add to it as you go along or reorganize it to better fit your needs.

Your aim is to create a working model of what you want or expect your business to do. As you track the numbers, you have reasons for the decisions and assumptions you make. You may forget these reasons as you plow through the projection process, so annotate.

Be alert to timing. As you work through your P&L projection line by line, keep asking yourself what changes you want to make and when you plan to implement those changes. If you plan to move to more spacious quarters, when? What added costs are involved? What other expenses will be affected? If you'll be mounting a major marketing program in the fall, you don't spread it through the entire year. You add it to the expected marketing expenses at the time you incur the expense. You may also be replacing one cost with another. You don't want to separate the expense from the period in which the expense was incurred.

If this seems confusing, don't lose heart. Get help. The important thing about the projected P&L is that it embodies your ideas. Your CPA or financial advisor can grind out the numbers for you. But you must understand how those numbers were arrived at or know where to find out.

Whenever you put a forecast or projection together, the notes are an important part of the total package. You don't have to share them with your investors, but you should have them available for your own purposes. Over time, they provide a valuable resource for ideas, reasoning, and arguments over goals and direction.

▶ Sales Forecast

This Aardvark Inc. example is for an ongoing business.

Sales Category Projections

Segment	2011		2012
			Most Likely
Safety	$375,000	0.24	$400,000
Overstock	$130,000	0.08	$145,000
Recreational Marine	$535,000	0.34	$625,000
Traditional Rigging	$285,000	0.18	$350,000
Outdoors/Camping	$235,000	0.15	$275,000
Totals	**$1,560,000**	**1.00**	**$1,795,000**

2011 Historical Data

2011 Total By Month	Jan	Feb	Mar	Total	
Safety	$31,400	$18,750	$18,750	$68,900	
Overstock	$85,000	$10,000	$2,000	$97,000	
Recreational Marine	$42,800	$26,750	$26,750	$96,300	
Traditional Rigging	$22,800	$14,250	$14,250	$51,300	
Outdoors/Camping	$18,800	$11,750	$11,750	$42,300	
Monthly total	**$200,800**	**$81,500**	**$73,500**	**$355,800**	
Cum. Monthly total	**$200,800**	**$282,300**	**$355,800**		

2011 Total By Quarter	1st	2nd	3rd	4th	Total
Safety	$68,900	$120,000	$100,000	$87,500	$376,400
Overstock	$97,000	$3,000	$3,000	$27,000	$130,000
Recreational Marine	$96,300	$200,000	$145,700	$93,000	$535,000
Traditional Rigging	$51,300	$85,000	$95,000	$55,000	$286,300
Outdoors/Ramping	$42,300	$75,000	$75,000	$40,000	$232,300
Total	**$355,800**	**$483,000**	**$418,700**	**$302,500**	**$1,560,000**
% Annual Sales	23%	31%	27%	19%	100%

2012 Sales Projections

2012 Total By month	Jan	Feb	Mar	Total	
Safety	$36,110	$21,563	$21,563	$79,235	
Overstock	$97,750	$11,500	$2,300	$111,550	
Recreational Marine	$49,220	$30,763	$30,763	$110,745	
Traditional Rigging	$26,220	$16,388	$16,388	$58,995	
Outdoors/Camping	$21,620	$13,513	$13,513	$48,645	
Monthly Total	**$230,920**	**$93,725**	**$84,525**	**$409,170**	
Cum. Monthly Total	**$230,920**	**$324,645**	**$409,170**		
	13%	5%	5%	23%	

2012 Total By Quarter	1st	2nd	3rd	4th	Total
Safety	$79,235	$138,000	$115,000	$100,625	$432,860
Overstock	$111,550	$3,450	$3,450	$31,050	$149,500
Recreational Marine	$110,745	$230,000	$167,555	$106,950	$615,250
Traditional Rigging	$58,995	$97,750	$109,250	$63,250	$329,245
Outdoors/Camping	$48,645	$86,250	$86,250	$46,000	$267,145
Total	**$409,170**	**$555,450**	**$481,505**	**$347,875**	**$1,794,000**
% Annual Sales	23%	31%	27%	19%	

▶ Projected P&L

Aardvark Inc.'s P&L is projected by month for the next year. Historical data is below, and 2012 projected P&L is on pages 148 and 149.

2011 Historical Data

		TOTALS	
Sales Revenue			
	Products	$1,561,350	
	Other	$0	
	Returns & Allowances	-$1,350	
Net Revenue		**$1,560,000**	
Cost Of Goods			
	Beg. Merchandise Inventory	$225,400	
	Net Purchases of Merchandise	$1,042,100	
	Ending Merchandise Inventory	$253,500	16.25%
Total COGS (V)		**$1,014,000**	**65.00%**
Gross Margin		**$546,000**	**35.00%**
Operating Expenses			
	Salaries etc. (F)	$283,650	18.18%
	Rent & Utilities (F)	$24,000	1.54%
	Insurance (F)	$12,000	0.77%
	Marketing & Advertising (F/V)	$30,000	1.92%
	Travel (V)	$8,000	0.51%
	Meals & Entertainment (V)	$3,000	0.19%
	Professional Fees (F)	$1,200	0.08%
	Telephone (F/V)	$6,000	0.38%
	Equipment Leases (F)	$3,600	0.23%
	Repairs & Maintenance (F)	$1,200	0.08%
	Amortization & Depreciation (F)	$23,550	1.51%
	Miscellaneous (F)	$1,750	0.11%
Total Operating Expenses		**$397,950**	**25.51%**
	EBIT	$148,050	9.49%
	Interest Expense (F)	$16,350	1.05%
Pretax Profit (Loss)		**$131,700**	**8.44%**
	Federal Taxes	$52,440	3.36%
	State Taxes		0.00%
Net Profit (Loss)		**$79,260**	**5.08%**

	A	B	C	D	E	F
1		Jan	Feb	Mar	Apr	May
2	**Sales Revenue**					
3	Products					
4	Other					
5	Returns & Allowances					
6	**Net Revenue**	230920	93725	84525	145000	185450
7						
8	**Cost Of Goods**					
9	Beg. Merchandise Inventory					
10	Net Purchases of Merchandise					
11	Ending Merchandise Inventory					
12						
13	**Total COGS (V)**	138552	56235	50715	87000	111270
14						
15	**Gross Margin**	92368	37490	33810	58000	74180
16						
17	**Operating Expenses**					
18	Salaries etc. (F)	27083	27000	27000	27000	27000
19	Rent & Utilities (F)	2500	2500	2500	2500	2500
20	Insurance (F)	1000	1000	1000	1000	1000
21	Marketing & Advertising (F/V)	3000	3000	12000	3000	3000
22	Travel (V)			3500		
23	Meals & Entertainment (V)			2000		
24	Professional Fees (F)	200	200	200	200	200
25	Telephone (F/V)	750	500	500	500	500
26	Equipment Leases (F)	300	300	300	300	300
27	Repairs & Maintenance (F)	150	150	150	150	150
28	Amortization & Depreciation (F)	1963	1963	1963	1963	1963
29	Miscellaneous (F)	200	200	200	200	200
30						
31	**Total Operating Expenses**	37146	36813	51313	36813	36813
32						
33	EBIT	55222	677	-17503	21188	37368
34						
35	Interest Expense (F)	1500	1500	1500	1500	1500
36						
37						
38	**Pretax Profit (Loss)**	53722	-823	-19003	19688	35868
39						
40	Federal Taxes					
41	State Taxes					
42						
43	**Net Profit (Loss)**	53722	-823	-19003	19688	35868

	G	H	I	J	K	L	M	N	O
1	Jun	Jul	Aug	Sep	Oct	Nov	Dec	TOTAL	
2									
3									
4									
5									
6	225000	185000	161500	135000	110000	53000	185000	1794120	
7									
8									
9									
10									
11									
12									
13	135000	111000	96900	81000	66000	31800	111000	1076472	
14									
15	90000	74000	64600	54000	44000	21200	74000	717648	
16									
17									
18	27000	27000	27000	27000	27000	27000	27000	324083	
19	2500	2500	2500	2500	2500	2500	2500	30000	
20	1250	1250	1250	1250	1250	1250	1250	13750	
21	6000	3000	3000	3000	3000	3000	3000	48000	
22		2500			1000			7000	
23		1000			500			3500	
24	200	200	200	200	200	200	200	2400	
25	750	500	500	500	500	500	500	6500	
26	300	500	500	500	500	500	500	4800	
27	150	150	150	150	150	150	150	1800	
28	1963	1963	1963	1963	1963	1963	1963	23551	
29	200	200	200	200	200	200	200	2400	
30									
31	40313	40763	37263	37263	38763	37263	37263	467784	
32									
33	49688	33238	27338	16738	5238	-16063	36738	249864	
34									
35	1500	1500	1500	1500	1500	1500	1500	18000	
36									
37									
38	48188	31738	25838	15238	3738	-17563	35238	231864	13%
39									
40									
41									
42									
43	48188	31738	25838	15238	3738	-17563	35238	231864	

Items on the Projected P&L

References are to rows and (columns). For example, **7(A)** refers to row 7, column A.

▶ **6(A) Net Revenue:** Sales are entered the month they are booked. They could all come in on the first or last day of the month. Note that sales may or may not be cash. Aardvark's credit sales are all Net 30. In this example, the sales pattern is derived from Aardvark's experience. They have had a steady history of 15 percent of sales being cash (or credit or debit cards that are treated as cash), 85 percent on terms. Aardvark's returns and allowances are nil, so we just show the Net Revenue. If returns and allowances are an important factor in your business, work returns and allowances into your forecast.

▶ **13(A) Total Cost of Goods Sold:** This is one of the most important figures for running your business. Some professional and other services have extremely low COGS, as they sell time rather than a product and might only include a few items they sell their clients. A hairdresser who sells brushes and shampoos would have a COGS; a hairdresser who only sells haircuts and styling would not. Check with your accountant. Aardvark sells products (merchandise). For reasons of simplicity, we show only the Total COGS. Note: COGS is a variable cost.

▶ **15(A) Gross Margin:** This is the most important single figure to follow, as it reflects both sales and COGS. This is what pays the operating expenses and provides a margin for profitability.

▶ **17(A) Operating Expenses:** These include fixed and variable expenses. Fixed expenses, the proverbial nut, mostly come due monthly. These are marked by (F). Variable expenses (marked by (V) or (V/F)) go up or down with sales.

▶ **18(A) Salaries plus Benefits:** These run 20 to 30 percent of salaries and are a big expense. Although some months have three pay periods, this is figured as if each month were the same. If major raises are anticipated in (for example) August, you would increase this line at that time.

▶ **19(A) Rent and Utilities:** Aardvark's rent and utilities go up from $2,000/month to $2,500/month on January 1, 2011. Utilities are paid at a flat rate and are included in the lease.

▶ **20(A) Insurance:** Insurance is paid quarterly, but the expense is spread monthly. Note the increase in June.

▶ **21(A) Marketing and advertising:** Aardvark has a complex marketing and advertising figure. It's part fixed (mainly for newspaper and magazine advertisements) and part variable. In March and June they have added marketing and advertising costs associated with trade shows, a vital aspect of their plans to increase sales and drive down COGS.

The costs are accrued sporadically; the benefits accrue steadily. Although this is a variable, treat it as a fixed expense for budgeting purposes on the theory that you've invested heavily to gain a market presence and will fight to retain it. Even if sales were down you'd continue to fund this item at the projected rate. If possible, you'd invest more than budgeted.

▶ **22(A) Travel:** Travel varies with the season, and is tied to marketing and trade shows. (See **22(D)**: attendance at a major trade show reflects the deviation.)

▶ **23(A) Meals and entertainment:** Aardvark's meals and entertainment expenses are also tied to trade shows.

▶ **24(A) Professional fees:** These are paid quarterly during the year, but their benefit accrues throughout the year. This expense covers accounting and legal advice.

▶ **25(A) Telephone:** This is another mixed expense. Treat it as fixed to be conservative.

▶ **26(A) Equipment leases:** Equipment leases for copier and some other electronics.

▶ **27(A) Repairs and maintenance:** This is a minor expense. Aardvark has to keep premises tidy and machinery working.

▶ **28(A) Amortization and depreciation:** This is a non-cash expense on more than half a million dollars of PP&E (Plant, Property and Equipment). No change is expected from last year though the accountant might advise otherwise. If so, it will be adjusted.

Depreciation is used to lower taxable revenue. Some experts swear that Amortization & Depreciation is the last, best tax loophole. Depreciation writes down the cost of some tangible assets, while amortization does the same for intangible assets such as good will.

▶ **29(A) Miscellaneous:** Miscellaneous expenses cover paperclips, other office supplies, miscellaneous postage, and odds and ends. This should be a very low number.

▶ **31(A):** This is the total of all the operating expenses.

▶ **33(A) EBIT:** This stands for Earnings Before Interest and Taxes. This figure shows the real cost of operations, interest, and taxes. While major expenses, they are not operating expenses.

▶ **35(A) Interest payments:** Interest expenses on equipment loans, term loan for working capital, and a line of credit. Note that this is interest only. Principal repayments show up on the cash flows pro forma.

▶ **38(A) Pre-tax profit:** This is the measure of the efficiency of the business. This is a better measure than the after-tax profit or loss. Your tax burden is largely a function of your accountant's skill. Be glad you're making a profit to be taxed on. Be worried if you're not.

▶ **40(A) Federal tax:** Corporate income taxes vary from year to year depending on the whims of the IRS and the skill of the accountant.

▶ **41(A) New Hampshire business profit tax:** The accountant will figure this out. Legislation is currently in flux.

▶ **43(A) Cumulative profit (loss) pre-tax:** Use this to compare this year's performance to historical data. Spot trends. See Variance Analysis in Chapter 25.

H1 P&L Forecasting

The governing rules in preparing a P&L forecast are:

1. **Don't sweat the small stuff.** While you want to be accurate, there's a point of diminishing returns that you reach quickly. Don't agonize over spreading a minor item such as the telephone bill, which is part variable, part fixed.

2. **On large numbers, think it through.** That's why the sales forecast was so detailed. You're trying to establish major guidelines. You can't include everything. Just as a baseball manager looks first at the batting averages, ERAs, won/loss record, and the like before turning to finer measures, you want to be able to swiftly check your company's progress.

That means riding herd on revenues, margin, and profit or loss.

3. **Use your computer to grind out the calculations and spare you much of the drudgery of spreadsheet analysis.**

4. **Customize your P&L to your own uses.** For some entries, one line is more informative than six. Greater detail doesn't always lead to better information transfer.

5. **Your projected P&Ls should have the same format and entries as your monthly P&L.** Otherwise you'll waste time shuffling numbers from the monthlies to some other format.

Once you get the hang of making a projection, the actual time involved is minimal. The effort before the projection is where time mounts up, as you think through the initial goals and sales forecasts. Perhaps 90 percent of your time will be spent on these initial steps.

Two- to Five-Year P&L Projections

You'll use the 12-month projection to run your business. You use the two- to five-year projections as a polestar to keep you more or less on course as you strive to reach long-term objectives. Review the 12-month forecast every six months or so, more often if you're in a transitional or fast-growth business. You never implement the long-range projections. They keep receding, serving a useful and important learning function, but never being actually applied.

Quarterly projections for years two through five (and their annotations) are similar to the monthly projections. The main difference is detail. Five-year forecasts are less detailed, essentially an extrapolation of past and current growth, tempered as always by your knowledge and experience. The five-year forecast is built on sales forecasts which themselves are extrapolations and estimates of what will probably happen. Don't get swamped in details. In particular, the operating expenses should be made as simple as possible.

23

The Pro Forma Cash Flow

Cash flow pro formas (cash budgets) help you decide what your debt and capital needs are, what their timing should be, and whether you can afford to be in business. This may be the single most valuable tool at your disposal. An old business saying is that any fool can make a budget, but it takes a skilled owner/manager to set a good budget.

Positive cash flow equals survival. It buys time (if necessary), builds assets and profits, and keeps suppliers, bankers, creditors, and investors smiling. With negative cash flow, survival becomes questionable. Negative or feebly positive cash flow is painful and, unless corrected, will either kill a business or damage it so seriously that it never lives up to its potential. While short periods of negative cash flow occur in almost every business, cash flows have to be positive at least on an annual basis. Some farmers do very well indeed with cash flows that are strongly negative for 11 months of the year. So do some manufacturers (especially in the garment trade). The key is that they know what their cash flow patterns are—and take steps to finance the negative periods, offsetting that cost against the occasional strong positive cash influx from operations. Unfortunately, the smaller and more thinly capitalized the company, the less able it is to survive extended negative cash flows. This is one reason why so many startups fail. The business idea may be terrific, but sales always come more slowly than expected, while cash goes out twice as fast. And the initial investment is rarely enough to tide the business along until cash flow turns and stays positive. How can a small business attain positive cash flow? Discipline.

A cash flow budget is an unbeatable tool if followed carefully. The concept of "profit" is so pervasive that it poses a barrier to understanding that positive cash flow does not equal profit (or vice versa). The example of a profitable growing company with negative cash flow succumbing to illiquidity and tumbling into Chapter 11 is commonly cited to disprove the notion. If the sales don't turn to cash soon enough, the company goes broke. Revenues are up, receivables are up, expenses are up, and profits are up. Yet the company runs out of cash, can't pay its bills, and becomes another cash flow victim. Another conceptual problem is equating P&L losses with negative cash flow. While a loss on the P&L can reflect a negative cash flow, it doesn't have to.

If you have only one financial statement, have it be the cash flow pro forma. Cash flow budgets have kept many businesses going until their management acquires more financial skills. A cash flow teaches liquidity (cash availability), which is more important to survival than profitability. How can you run an unprofitable business? By maintaining a positive cash flow. While this won't last forever, because ulti-

---

T

▶ Cash Flow

Dickens' Mr. Micawber put it best in *David Copperfield*: "Annual income twenty pounds, annual expenditure nineteen six, result happiness. Annual income twenty pounds, annual expenditure twenty pounds ought and six, result misery." Dickens was right. He understood cash flow. In essence, happiness equals a positive cash flow. For small businesses, positive cash flow equals survival. In the long run you must make an operating profit (the main source of cash), but at least in the short run cash flow is more important.

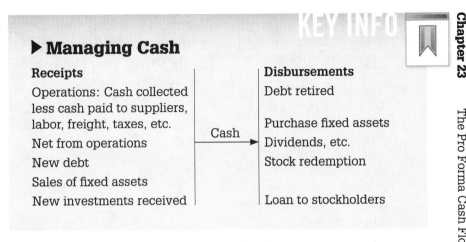

▶ Managing Cash

Receipts		Disbursements
Operations: Cash collected less cash paid to suppliers, labor, freight, taxes, etc.		Debt retired
	Cash	Purchase fixed assets
Net from operations		Dividends, etc.
New debt		Stock redemption
Sales of fixed assets		
New investments received		Loan to stockholders

mately cash flow and profitability are closely related, it can paper over short-term gaps. Companies without cash flow budgets invariably run into liquidity and solvency problems: they run out of cash.

The cash flow projection (pro forma cash budget) is the most important single statement for controlling your business. A cash budget controls the dribbles that bleed a business: An unnecessary purchase here, an unwise hire there, a small donation to a worthy cause. The dribbles soon amount to a gusher, and plugging that outflow is extraordinarily difficult.

The cash flow is concerned with money in motion, the actual flow of cash through your business. While the P&L is modified to a degree by timing, in the cash flow (CF) timing is all-important. When does a sale turn into cash? When does a bill get paid? When do you receive a loan? The proceeds of a new investment? The underlying questions are: When? How much?

If you have been realistic in your sales forecasting and P&L projections, the mechanics of preparing your cash flow pro forma are not difficult.

Cash Flow Pro Forma

The cash flow pro forma starts with cash inflows from operations. Sales drive every business and if you're going to raise new investment money, new debt, or stay in business, you must make an operating profit. This is only possible if sales revenues exceed expenses.

The format of the cash flow pro forma (explanations of each number in brackets follows the pro forma):

KEY INFO

▶ Sample Format for Cash Flow Pro Forma

[1]   Cash Inflows
         Cash Sales
         Cash From Receivables
         Other Cash Sources
[2]   Subtotal: Cash From Operations
[3]   Proceeds of Loan
[4]   New Investment
[5]   Other
[6]   Total Cash In
[7]   Cash Disbursements:
[8]   Variable Disbursements
[9]   Fixed Disbursements
[10]   Other
[11]   Total Cash Disbursements
[12]   Cash Flow
[13]   Cumulative Cash Flow
[14]   Cash at Start of Period
     +   Cash Inflow
     −   Cash Outflow
     =   Cash at End of Period

Items on the Cash Flow Pro Forma

[1]   When you receive cash makes a big difference. Cash always comes in more slowly than you hope and flows out faster. If all of your sales are cash sales, you can focus on the disbursements (after copying the sales forecast month by month). For the majority of businesses, extending credit to customers is a fact of life. If your customers buy from you now and pay you later this pattern must be reflected in your cash flow.

[2]   Operations is the primary source of cash. All of the other sources depend on a steady flow of cash from operations, which is operating profit corrected for receivables timing. The "Other" operating cash can be anything from secondary cash sources (proceeds of investments, interest on deposit accounts being common) to refunds of taxes. Tax refunds can be significant sources of cash, but you have to have made the payment in the first place.

[3], [4], [5] These are self-explanatory. You borrow money and cash comes in. You or someone else invests in the business and cash comes in. "Other" includes sales of fixed assets, proceeds of lawsuits settled in your favor, or other non-operating cash inflows.

[6] All cash inflows for the period. Sum of **[2]**, **[3]**, **[4]**, and **[5]**.

[7] Cash Disbursements do not equal expenses. Disbursements for the cash flow involve the cash you actually shell out (amount and timing). You may incur an expense but take your time about paying it. You don't disburse any cash until you send the check or cash.

[8] Variable disbursements correspond to the variable expenses on the P&L. You enter them as they're paid, not before. You have considerable latitude in when to make your payments, subject to the good will and tolerance of your suppliers and other creditors.

[9] Fixed disbursements correspond to fixed expenses. This is the nut, the cash that you pay out no matter how high or low sales are. This does not include amortization and depreciation or non-cash expenses.

[10] Variable and fixed costs are operating expenses transmogrified into disbursements. "Other" includes any other non-operating use of cash: loans to stockholders, dividends, stock repurchase, principal payments on loans, or purchase of fixed assets are examples.

[11] All cash outflows for the period. The sum of **[8]**, **[9]** and **[10]**.

[12] **[12]** Cash flow = **[6]** Cash inflows – **[11]** Cash outflows. If this figure is positive, you enjoy positive cash flow. If it is negative, you suffer negative cash flow.

[13] Cumulative cash flow: add current month cash flow to the sum of the previous months' cash flows. Some forms add a space for cash flow from operations. However, very few small businesses use this kind of analysis, as non-operating disbursements and inflows tend to be rare, small, or both. Loans are usually for operating purposes such as inventory or equipment, and lawsuit awards are unusual.

Projecting a cash flow involves the usual conflict between detail and overload. You want to make sure the sales forecast, recast in the cash flow, is accurate, but you don't want to get bogged down in too much fine-tuning.

T MORE

▶ Projecting Cash Flow For Aardvark Inc.

[1] $\dfrac{\text{Net Sales}}{\text{Avg. Trade Receivables}}$ = Number of Receivables Turns Per Year

[2] $\dfrac{365}{\text{Receivables Turn}}$ = Avg. Age of Receivables

Aardvark's 2011 sales were $1,560,000, and receivables averaged $145,200, so there were 10.7 turns for an average of 21 days. In other words, non-cash sales turn to cash, on average, 21 days later:

[3] 1560000/145200   = 10.7 (turns)
[4] 365/10.7   = 34 (days)

These use projected values for Aardvark 2012:
[1] Annual Sales   = $1,795,000
[2] Average Receivables   = $155,000
[3] Total Credit Sales
   (Average receivables) x 12   = $1,860,000
[4] Receivables Turn
   (Annual Sales)/(Avg. Receivables) = 11.4 times
[5] Average Age of Receivables
   365/(Receivables Turn)   = 32 days

Credit and collection patterns tend to be stable. Since you track receivables, you already have a good grasp of the age and importance of your receivables. (See Chapter 17, Ratio Analysis, for more.) Following the example, each month's forecasted sales will turn to cash in the following month. The average age of receivables is 32 days. Keep in mind that receivables have a nasty habit of growing old. This is an area for Aardvark to work on but it represents an improvement from 2011's 34 days.

You might wonder if the next step would be to add whatever numbers might be appropriate for new debt or new investment. The answer depends on how you plan to use the cash flow. If the new debt or new investment is already secure, the answer is yes. You would want to measure its impact on your cash flow. However, you may want to get a line on your operating cash needs— including new debt and new capital—first. The best way to do this is to work through your variable and fixed disbursements next. This will allow you to figure when you'll hit a negative cash position and decide how to resolve the problem.

Cash In

In this example (See Aardvark's 2012 CF pro forma on pages 162 and 163), total cash from operations is $1,773,720, while sales for the same period are forecast as $1,794,000. The difference is due to revenue coming in from the previous December 2011 ($136,850) and being deferred from December 2012 ($157,250). The difference is $27,730, which corresponds to the difference between forecast sales and forecast cash from operations.

References are to rows and (columns). For example, **7(A)** refers to row 7, column A.

- ▶ **7(A) Cash from operations:** Track this month to month.
- ▶ **9(A), 10(A)** Leave these lines blank for now. Once you've completed your cash flow, you'll know what you have to finance (and when you need financing). At that time, you'll return to these lines. They exemplify use of the cash flow in managing by the numbers. If you plan to buy a fixed asset or make a capital investment, this is where you would put the proposed expenditure.

	A	B	C	D	E	F
1	**Cash Flow Pro Forma**	**Jan**	**Feb**	**Mar**	**Apr**	**May**
2	Cash Inflows					
3	Cash Sales	$34,638	$14,059	$12,679	$21,750	$27,818
4	Cash From Receivables	$136,850	$196,282	$79,666	$71,846	$123,250
5	Other Cash Sources					
6						
7	Subtotal Cash From Operations	$171,488	$210,341	$92,345	$93,596	$151,068
8						
9	Proceeds Of Loan					
10	New Investment					
11	Other					
12	Total Cash In	$171,488	$210,341	$92,345	$93,596	$151,068
13						
14	Cash Disbursements:					
15	Variable Disbursements					
16	COGS	$195,000		$148,985		$342,000
17	Travel			$3,500		
18	Meals & Entertainment			$2,000		
19	Total Variable Disbursements	$195,000	$-	$154,485	$-	$342,000
20	Fixed Disbursements					
21	Salaries, Etc.	$25,000	$25,000	$37,500	$25,000	$25,000
22	Rent & Utilities	$2,500	$2,500	$2,500	$2,500	$2,500
23	Marketing & Advertising	$3,000	$3,000	$12,000	$3,000	$3,000
24	Insurance		$3,000			$3,000
25	Professional Fees	$200	$200	$200	$200	$200
26	Telephone	$750	$500	$500	$500	$500
27	Equipment Leases	$300	$300	$300	$300	$300
28	Repairs & Maintenance	$150	$150	$150	$150	$150
29	Miscellaneous	$200	$200	$200	$200	$200
30	Other					
31	Total Fixed Disbursements	$32,100	$34,850	$53,350	$31,850	$34,850
32	Total Op. Cash Disbursements	$227,100	$34,850	$207,835	$31,850	$376,850
33	Principal Repayments	$12,000			$12,000	
34	Interest			$4,500		
35	Total P&I	$12,000	$-	$4,500	$12,000	$-
36	Taxes					
37	Federal Income Tax					
38	State Income Tax					
30	Total Taxes:	$-	$-	$-	$-	$-
40	**Total Cash Disbursements**	**$239,100**	**$34,850**	**$212,335**	**$43,850**	**$376,850**
41						
42	**Cash Flow**	**$(67,612)**	**$175,491**	**$(119,990)**	**$49,746**	**$(225,783)**
43						
44	**Cumulative Cash Flow**	**$(67,612)**	**$107,879**	**$(12,111)**	**$37,635**	**$(188,148)**
45						
46	Cash At Start of Period	97950	$30,338	$205,829	$85,839	$135,585
47	Add Cash Receipts	$171,488	$210,341	$92,345	$93,596	$151,068
48	Subtract Cash Disbursements	$239,100	$34,850	$212,335	$43,850	$376,850
49	Cash At End of Period	$30,338	$205,829	$85,839	$135,585	$(90,198)

	G	H	I	J	K	L	M	N
1	Jun	Jul	Aug	Sep	Oct	Nov	Dec	TOTAL
2								
3	$33,750	$27,750	$24,225	$20,250	$16,500	$7,950	$27,750	$269,118
4	$157,633	$191,250	$157,250	$137,275	$114,750	$93,500	$45,050	$1,504,602
5								
6								
7	$191,383	$219,000	$181,475	$157,525	$131,250	$101,450	$72,800	$1,773,720
8								
9								
10								
11								
12	191,383	219,000	181,475	157,525	131,250	101,450	72,800	1,773,720
13								
14								
15								
16		$147,000			$142,800		$225,000	$1,200,785
17		$2,500			$1,000			$7,000
18		$1,000			$500			$3,500
19	$-	$150,500	$-	$-	$144,300	$-	$225,000	$1,211,285
20								$-
21	$25,000	$25,000	$25,000	$25,000	$37,500	$25,000	$27,000	$327,000
22	$2,500	$2,500	$2,500	$2,500	$2,500	$2,500	$2,500	$30,000
23	$6,000	$3,000	$3,000	$3,000	$3,000	$3,000	$3,000	$48,000
24			$3,750			$3,750		$13,500
25	$200	$200	$200	$200	$200	$200	$200	$2,400
26	$750	$500	$500	$500	$500	$500	$500	$6,500
27	$300	$500	$500	$500	$500	$500	$500	$4,800
28	$150	$150	$150	$150	$150	$150	$150	$1,800
29	$200	$200	$200	$200	$200	$200	$200	$2,400
30								$-
31	$35,100	$32,050	$35,800	$32,050	$44,550	$35,800	$34,050	$436,400
32	$35,100	$182,550	$35,800	$32,050	$188,850	$35,800	$259,050	$1,647,685
33		$12,000			$12,000			$48,000
34	$4,500			$4,500	$-		$4,500	$18,000
35	$4,500	$12,000	$-	$4,500	$12,000	$-	$4,500	$66,000
36								$-
37								$-
38								$-
39	$-	$-	$-	$-	$-	$-	$-	$-
40	$39,600	$194,550	$35,800	$36,550	$200,850	$35,800	$263,550	$1,713,685
41								
42	$151,783	$24,450	$145,675	$120,975	$(69,600)	$65,650	$(190,750)	$60,035
43								
44	$(36,365)	$(11,915)	$133,760	$254,735	$185,135	$250,785	$60,035	
45								
46	$(90,198)	$61,585	$86,035	$231,710	$352,685	$283,085	$348,735	$157,985
47	$191,383	$219,000	$181,475	$157,525	$131,250	$101,450	$72,800	$1,773,720
48	$39,600	$194,550	$35,800	$36,550	$200,850	$35,800	$263,550	$1,713,685
49	$61,585	$86,035	$231,710	$352,685	$283,085	$348,735	$157,985	

▶ **12(A) Total cash in:** the sum of operations and new debt and investment.

Cash Out

Now to the cash disbursement side of the equation. The easiest place to start is with the fixed disbursements, since they can easily be isolated and entered. These are absolutely predictable disbursements, with fixed amounts and timing. Some of the figures will be rounded off. The aim is to present an accurate picture of the entire company's cash flow, with special accuracy on the larger cash items.

▶ **21(A)** In the P&L, salaries included FICA, benefits, and similar items. For purposes of the cash flow, more detail may be handy. It's all too easy to mess up taxes—easy and expensive. Withholding taxes are included in salaries, which have been rounded off to reflect pay schedules. March and October are three payperiod months, the rest have two payperiods.

▶ **22(A) Rent and utilities:** Utilities are higher in winter, lower in summer, but Aardvark uses a flat pay plan.

▶ **23(A)** Treat **marketing and advertising** as a fixed cost, although they're derived as a percentage of projected sales. This will provide continuity in your promotional efforts. Rather than slashing marketing and advertising during slow periods, or cutting them to improve apparent profitability during good periods, you'll find a consistent approach works best. In this example we budget 15% of projected annual sales. Roughly half goes into ongoing "presence" efforts, half into special mailings, trade shows, and other erratic expenditures. Keep this figure on a cash basis (see the P&L projection), as it's paid as incurred. While this obscures some of the cash flow of actual marketing and advertising disbursements, some of the disbursements can be arranged to suit our convenience.

▶ **24(A) Insurance** is paid quarterly, increases in August.

▶ **25(A) Professional fees** are paid quarterly.

▶ **26(A) Telephone** is paid thirty days after receiving service.

▶ **27(A)** Payments on **leased equipment**.

▶ **28(A) Repair and maintenance** goes up and down, too small to schedule.

▶ **29(A) Miscellaneous;** petty cash items.

▶ **30(A)** Other, non-operating costs.

Variable Disbursements

The next step in preparing the CF is to spread the variable disbursements. Since we're interested in when these disbursements are made as well as the amounts, we can't simply multiply cash inflows from operations by an even percentage each month, except in the limiting case of an all-cash business.

▶ **16(A) Cost of goods sold:** the largest variable expense for most retailers and manufacturers. This is another key figure to track monthly.

▶ **17(A) Travel:** This is mainly for trade shows and education.

▶ **18(A) Meals and entertainment** are considered variable disbursements but don't have a regular percentage of sales as their base. Instead, they're tied to ongoing activities and occasional major trade shows. These are "plugged" figures based on estimated outlays.

Finalizing the CF

At this stage the CF is almost finished. All the major disbursements, both fixed and variable, have been identified, including **31(A)** and **32(A)**.

▶ **33(A) and 34(A):** Separate principal repayments and interest as they are not operating costs.

▶ **35(A) Total P&I:** Sum of taxes paid.

▶ **37(A) and 38(A):** These are for federal and state taxes. They're left open until the accountant can provide a figure.

▶ **40(A) Total cash disbursements:** the sum of **(32)** Total operating cash disbursements, **(35)** Total P&I, and **(40)** Total Taxes.

▶ **42(A) Cash flow:** Subtract operating cash disbursements, Total P&I, and Total Taxes from Total cash inflows **(12)** to arrive at Cash flow. In the example, cash flow is volatile. It's positive for the total year in spite of a large inventory purchase in December.

▶ **44(A) Cumulative cash flow:** Jan + Feb + Mar + ... + Dec. The cumulative cash flow tends to balance out the inevitable slopping about of some of the figures. It starts negative in January, positive in February, negative in March, positive in April, strongly negative in May, mildly negative in June and July, before turning positive for the rest of the year. This fits the sales and revenue patterns of this business. Since they know in advance that cash will be scarce in May, management can plot a strategy to minimize the impact. Perhaps ask for a prepayment, seek additional capital, lean on trade a bit, or call for an inventory loan. These are investment decisions yet to be made.

▶ Operating Cash Flow

Operating cash flow is figured by subtracting variable and fixed disbursements from cash from operations. This cleans out non-operating sources and uses of cash and provides an operating cash budget. Many business owners find this an especially helpful figure and also prepare a similar operating P&L budget. The aim is to answer the question of whether operations are generating or eating cash. You hope for generation of cash, as that's the engine that drives your business.

▶ **46(A) to 49(A)** This projects the cash position, based on the pro forma cash flow. Aardvark started the year with $97,950 on hand and would potentially end up with $157,985. In real life this wouldn't be allowed to happen. The cash would be reinvested in the business to generate growth, retire debt, purchase new equipment, or other fixed assets. Or, for a temporary measure, be parked in an interest-bearing deposit account.

Cash Flow Five-Year Projections

Long-range cash flow projections are less useful than the P&L five-year projections. Their main use is to identify capital needs if the short-term (one-year) cash flow has not turned positive. For most businesses the main reason to prepare a long-term cash flow projection is to satisfy investor or banker demands. It can also be used to understand the potential impact on the company of major investments or divestitures. Most financial proposals will include a three- or five-year cash flow pro forma to show how an investment will pay off. Your accountant or other financial advisor should help you make sure that the numbers hang together, but once again, it's your ideas and insights that are expressed (or should be) in the five-year projections.

If you need to prepare long-range cash flows, follow this procedure:

1. **Start with the long-range P&L forecast.** This contains most of the information needed in preparing your cash flow quarterlies for years two through five.

2. **As in the earlier cash flow, the cash inflows will consist of cash sales, conversion of accounts receivable to cash, new investment, new debt, and the proceeds of the sale of fixed assets.** The timing of the first two is less critical than in the one-year pro forma because most receivables, for most companies, don't stretch out much beyond 90 days—that is, all sales become cash within the quarter. If you have an erratic sales pattern and a long receivables return, your particular timing has to be shown.

3. **Timing of new debt, new equity investment, or the proceeds of sales of fixed assets (including sale of a division or profit center) are important.** Long-range plans, particularly if they will be used to raise new capital, focus on the impact of such cash inflows. The long-term P&L forecast will have shown how they impact profitability. The cash flow pro forma shows how the plan will be implemented and liquidity problems avoided.

4. **On the disbursement side, the fixed vs. variable distinctions remain important, but less detail needs to be shown.** The three- or five-year pro forma is not concerned with minutia. While considerable detail is necessary in the one-year pro forma because it will be used as a budget, the long-term concern is just this: will the company become illiquid under the assumptions underlying the pro forma?

5. **Keep notes.** Whether or not the plans are implemented, the notes will help you understand your business better.

Using the Cash Flow

The cash flow provides monthly cash budget figures, which if well-based, are the best standards you can have to help you manage your business. If you pick up nothing else from this book than how to set standards and try to achieve them, you'll be in better shape than most businesses.

One of the most important uses of the cash flow, especially for startups and businesses in transition, is to establish capital needs. It's the best way to anticipate other financing needs, including when to prepare proposals to present to banks or other investors (yourself included) to help them reach their (your) decisions. Use this early-warning system to build your credibility with your banker. A timely proposal will invariably be better received than a panicky request for funds, right now, to meet payroll or cover taxes.

For Startups and Transitional Businesses

Capital needs are roughly determined by the magnitude of negative cash flows. As you either start or redirect a business in transition, you will face periods of negative cash flows and must have a strategy in place to counteract those outflows.

Most small businesses are undercapitalized. Everyone hopes to generate enough operating profit to grow his or her way out of undercapitalization (by retaining earnings), but this is usually not possible. Growth eats cash faster than it generates cash, so except for the patient (or the fortunate: you may have major customers who will fund your growth by prepayment), more capital will be required. Bankers watch the Debt-to-Net Worth ratio closely, so financing your way through startup or transition may not be a possibility. As a rule of thumb, a Debt-to-Net Worth ratio in excess of 2:1 will shut off new credit.

That leaves invested capital as the primary source of funds in these businesses.

How much capital do you need and when will you need it? If your projections show a substantial cumulative negative cash flow and the monthly cash flows have not turned positive, continue the cash flow until your business shows a consistent positive cash flow. If your pro formas go out more than two years with consistently negative or only sporadically positive cash flows, sit down with your advisors. Your business plans must change or you should shut the doors now and avoid future cash drain. This is extraordinarily valuable advice to heed. Remember: survival equals positive cash flow.

The Doubling Rule of Capital

If the cash flow is positive within twelve to eighteen months, look at the point of the greatest negative cumulative cash and then double this figure. That's the minimum amount of new capital needed.

Why double? Remember Murphy's Law: Whatever can go wrong will go wrong. You may find that a smaller amount will suffice or a combination of invested capital and debt or reserved capital will see you through, but it's prudent to line up cash while you can.

If the periods of negative cash flow are of a shorter duration, and the cumulative cash flow is positive, the cash flow will show you when to borrow, how much, and when and how you can pay it back without creating further cash flow problems. Look to the timing and amount of the cash flows. Ask your banker to help you determine the proper kind of credit (line of credit, receivables or inventory financing, or other). Bankers spend a lot of time learning how to finance small businesses, and your banker should be able to explain his or her reasoning.

Just having a cash flow pro forma will bathe your business in a favorable light. The cash flow (and the quarterlies for the next few years) illuminate seasonal credit needs and point out the need for additional working capital, which can often be financed by a bank.

Fast-Growth Businesses

Fast-growth businesses devour cash, pile up receivables, and run the risk of becoming illiquid. For such a business, there are only two possibilities: Slow down growth to harvest the profits from the sales, or get new investment into the business fast. The latter is normally the better route to pursue (unless a sales slowdown won't invite hungry competitors), but the amounts needed require a more sophisticated approach. Fortunately, if this is your problem, there are plenty of experts eager to help you calculate your capital needs.

You would use the cash flow (including quarterlies) to ascertain credit needs the same way any other business would. The difference is that your cash flow will undergo especially severe scrutiny, as the sums tend to be greater and the risks more substantial than in the other scenarios. That's why you want to consult experts. The stakes are too large to learn as you go.

Ongoing Businesses

For ongoing businesses, the cash flow is the heart of any financing proposal. You may want to use your most optimistic scenario rather than your most conservative scenario as the basis, but the moves are basically the same: negative cash flows call for more equity, more debt, or both, as well as some operational and strategic changes.

Persistent negative cash flows are a cause for alarm. The path to bankruptcy is foreshadowed by such negative cash flows. At the very least, the business plan should be rewritten and all the assumptions checked through.

Look for amounts, timing, and how the infusion of cash will be repaid.

The cash flow does more. Supposing there are no surprises in store, what else does it tell us? In the example, it shows that no added cash will be needed to stay solvent, provided we stick to it. If sales differ from projections, the cash flow helps us understand the impact.

24

The Budget and Beyond: Part Two of the Business Plan

Why should you create and manage to budgets?

Simple. Businesses that are run without budgets suffer chronic cash and vendor relation problems, don't thrive, and vanish sooner rather than later. The ideas behind a business may be terrific, the energy and commitment total, the customers supportive, but the discipline and control of establishing and then following a budget are needed to hold all of the pieces together. The trick has always been to establish a budget that reflects your business and its resources, opportunities, problems, and plans.

Financial management and control, and budgets are inseparable. The P&L and cash flow projections established earlier are the core of your budgets. For many small businesses the projections provide plenty of detail to manage the business well. Other businesses will want additional budgets, for example a separate marketing and advertising budget. A capital budget for major purchases such as plant and equipment is another useful tool. The purchase of capital assets is usually well-thought-out, but not always. It's too easy to get carried away by the excitement of new equipment.

You establish budgets for two reasons. First, you want to make sure that money is available when it's needed and that all expenditures further your company's business goals. Second, money has a penchant for dribbling away. A few dollars here and there can add up surprisingly fast and leave no trace. Leasing a copying machine may only cost $150/month. That's $1,800 a year, straight to the fixed cost column. If the expense was not budgeted because of the dubious rationale of "it's only $150/month," chances are it is not a justified expense.

If you make all disbursements by check, you at least have a record of where the money goes. If you make many checks out to cash, your records won't help you at all and the IRS will assess personal income taxes on you, as their reasonable presumption will be that these are personal expenses.

There are three ways to establish budgets: top down (imposed by management as a way to reach profit goals), bottom up, or collaborative. Each method has strong advocates. The larger the business, the more likely it is that the budget will be dictated from above, negotiated with the managers involved, and adhered to rigidly. That's why large businesses make large profits. They carefully craft their budgets and stick to them. Performance and salary reviews focus on how well or poorly managers hew to their assigned budgets.

Very small businesses often have no budgets at all, or have such fluid budgets that any excuse to violate them will be accepted. Such budgets as they do have tend to be a hodgepodge of ideas from all corners.

The compromise position, the collaborative budget, includes the managers in the budgeting process from the start. If you have only a few employees, this is far and away the best method to follow. You explain your goals, and your employees then help figure out how to attain them. Your employees will know the goals, see how the budget helps attain the goals, and will be less apt to resist budgetary constraints since they understand the reasoning.

A cash flow budget is always best for startups, businesses in transition, and fast-growth businesses concerned with liquidity and survival. Ongoing businesses prefer the P&L budget, as their interest is focused on profitability. In an ideal world you'd use both budgets on a monthly, rolling quarterly, and year-to-date basis. These methods are more fully explained in Chapter 25, Deviation Analysis.

The process is the same for each:

1. Establish the one-year forecast or pro forma.
2. Think through possible capital expenditures.
3. Examine financing needs and options.
4. Work capital expenditures and financing into the P&L and CF projections.

Establishing budgets is difficult. Making budgets effective and putting them to work is made easier by involving all key employees in the budgeting process from goal-setting through sales forecasts to the preliminary cash flow. Their insights strengthen the forecasts, add ideas you may have missed, and give them a sense of ownership of the numbers. This is vital. Otherwise managing to the budgets can degenerate into an unproductive argument about numbers that are meaningless to your employees, if not to you.

Budgets, Your Business Plan, and Your Financing Proposal

The first part of your business plan made clear what business you are in, what your products and markets are, who your competitors might be, and identifies key personnel and management. Now it's time to turn to the second part: the financials.

1. **The key historical financials are the balance sheet, the profit & loss, and the statement of cash flows for the preceding year.** You'll rarely need to delve further into the past but, being a diligent manager, you will have saved year-end financials for the past seven years to cover any problems with the IRS.
2. **You will definitely need projections and pro formas for your financing proposal, which is built on your business plan.** Bankers and other investors want to know what you've been doing recently, but they're even more interested in knowing what you plan to do going forward. You have to put the financial information into the format that they're familiar with, which is easy if your accountant is capable. But keep

in mind that the financials should reflect your thinking, not the accountant's.

3. **Your financing proposal should be a documented statement of what debt or equity you need, why you need it, and how you plan to repay it or provide a satisfactory return to the investor.** Documentation should include up-to-date balance sheets, cash flow pro formas, and projected P&Ls. All bankers have forms that help you prepare these, but by using your own business plan, you up your credibility.

4. **You should include a Sources & Applications statement (see below) to show what you will do with the new loans or equity.**

▶ Sources & Application of Financing

The Sources & Applications statement is a good summary of what you want the money for. Be prepared to defend it.

Use Of Funds	Amount Required	From Equity	From Loans
Acquire Building	$750,000	$500,000	$275,000
Improve Building	$240,000	$200,000	$40,000
Equipment	$100,00		$100,000

5. **Your proposal needs a contingency plan.** A contingency plan is a short worst-case business plan that examines the options that would be open to your business and how those options would be treated. Decisions made in panic are poor decisions. A contingency plan avoids panic (both yours and your banker's).

▶ Historical Financials Are Important

Historical financial statements are part of the business plan for several reasons:

▶ Businesses have a momentum that's difficult to alter.
▶ Past performance is an excellent, though not infallible, guide to future performance.

- ▶ Sales patterns established over years make planning easier and more accurate.
- ▶ They provide substantiation for projections.
- ▶ Bankers require them.

▶Financing Proposal

Your financing proposal should make clear:

1. How much money you want
2. What you want it for
3. What kind of money (debt, equity)
4. When you want it
5. Why it'll make your business better
6. How you'll pay it back
7. What your contingency plans might be—just in case

25

Managing by and to the Budget: Deviation Analysis

Deviation analysis measures actual performance against standards set by your budgets.

The process is more easily shown than described. Two variations are shown (monthly and year-to-date). A third variation uses "rolling quarters" in which you add the current month's actual performance to the two previous months' actual performance. This can smooth out month-to-month fluctuations, though this is a refinement you may not feel is necessary.

Use the cash flow monthly deviation and cash flow year-to-date deviation sheets for cash flow–based variance analysis, P&L monthly, and P&L year-to-date deviation sheets for P&L-based variance analysis. You choose which budget to follow. Ongoing businesses will ordinarily use P&L-based variance analysis effectively. Most other businesses benefit from the cash flow budget. However, the convenience of using a P&L budget may be the overriding factor. It's far better to follow a P&L budget than no budget at all. If you prepared both P&L-

based and cash flow–based budgets it is easy to use (and benefit from) both deviation analyses.

If you don't prepare monthly CF reports, use the P&L budget approach. Many small businesses don't bother to prepare monthly CF reports, though all (or almost all) do watch cash carefully. The important thing is that you have to adhere to your budget, because if you don't, expenses have a horrid habit of creeping up. If you don't at least attempt to follow your budget, there's no point in preparing forecasts or budgets.

Variance analysis is the easiest and most direct of all the financial management tools. Use your CF and P&L budgets to fill in column C, the projected or budgeted numbers.

The cash flow monthly deviation analysis and the P&L monthly deviation analysis sheets look like this:

TABLE

▶ Cash Flow Monthly Deviation Analysis

Monthly Report Cash Flow Deviation	A Actual Monthly	B Budget Monthly	C Deviation (B–A)	D % Deviation (C/B x 100)
Beginning Cash Balance				
Add				
Cash Sales				
Accounts Receivables That Have Turned to Cash				
Other Cash Inflows (Specify)				
Total Available Cash				
Estimated Disbursements				
Insurance				
Marketing & Advertising				
Travel				
Professional Fees				
Meals & Entertainment				
Loan Principal (Specify)				
Deduct Fixed Disbursements				
Salaries, etc.				
Rent & Utilities				
Telephone				

Equipment Leases				
Repairs & Maintenance				
Interest				
Total Disbursements				
Ending Cash Balance				

▶ P&L Monthly Deviation Analysis

Monthly Report P&L Deviation	A Actual	B Budget	C Deviation (B–A)	D % Deviation (C/B x 100)
Sales Revenue				
Products				
Other				
Returns & Allowances				
Net Revenue				
Cost of Goods				
Beginning Merchandise Inventory				
Net Purchases of Merchandise				
Ending Merchandise Inventory				
Total COGS				
Gross Margin				
Operating Expenses				
Salaries, etc. (F)				
Rent & Utilities (F)				
Insurance (F)				
Marketing & Advertising (F/V)				
Travel (V)				
Meals & Entertainment (V)				
Professional Fees (F)				
Telephone (F/V)				
Equipment Leases (F)				
Repairs & Maintenance (F)				

Amortization & Depreciation (F)				
Miscellaneous (F)				
Total Operating Expenses				
EBIT				
Interest Expense (F)				
Pretax Profit (Loss)				
Federal Taxes				
State Taxes				
Net Profit (Loss)				

The application of both of these analyses is the same.

1. Fill in column C, Projected performance.
2. Fill in column B, Actual performance.
3. Fill in column D, Deviation. This is calculated by subtracting B from C (D = C − B). This provides the absolute or dollar deviation.
4. The percent deviation of column E is calculated by the formula (D/C x 100). Sometimes the percent change is more important than the absolute dollar figure.

Investigate any deviation you consider significant. It may be an unpaid bill or an unexpected sale. Deviations can be good or bad. In either case, controlling your business depends on spotting these variances from the standards.

The monthly deviation analysis helps most with short-term deviations. Weather can affect sales, utilities, and other line items. The goal is to identify and understand the deviations, then take action if called for. Sometimes all you'll want to do is keep an eye on a deviation. That's a function of your judgment. Deviation analysis points out questions for you to ponder.

The YTD (year to date) projections and performance are arrived at by addition. January + February for February; January + February + March for March; and so forth.

The YTD deviation analysis accentuates trends, especially in the dollar deviation column. Since small amounts can become large over time, YTD is an important part of deviation analysis. YTD also helps smooth out the inevitable ups and downs that aren't unusual. A three-pay-period month, an unusual repair bill, a short spurt in sales can make the monthly numbers look peculiar. YTD tends to present a more balanced view of the actual performance of the business.

The main drawback to YTD is that it's based on the fiscal year, so for the first few months this smoothing effect is lacking. You can get around this by the "rolling quarters" method. In January, add last November and December to January projections. In February, add last December and the projections for January and February, and so on. You can continue this through the year, or abandon it once you have the patterns established. While this is a refinement, it helps prevent unnecessary worry over temporary blips, especially on the revenue side.

The YTD cash flow deviation and YTD P&L deviation sheets looks like this:

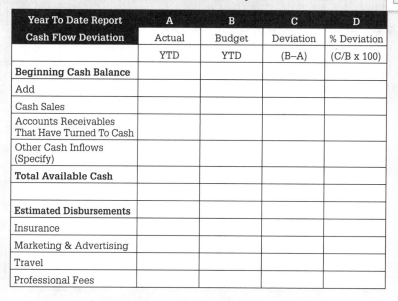

▶ Cash Flow YTD Deviation Analysis

Year To Date Report Cash Flow Deviation	A Actual	B Budget	C Deviation	D % Deviation
	YTD	YTD	(B–A)	(C/B x 100)
Beginning Cash Balance				
Add				
Cash Sales				
Accounts Receivables That Have Turned To Cash				
Other Cash Inflows (Specify)				
Total Available Cash				
Estimated Disbursements				
Insurance				
Marketing & Advertising				
Travel				
Professional Fees				

Meals & Entertainment				
Loan Principal (Specify)				
Deduct Fixed Disbursements				
Salaries, etc.				
Rent & Utilities				
Telephone				
Equipment Leases				
Repairs & Maintenance				
Interest				
Total Disbursements				
Ending Cash Balance				

▶ P&L Year To Date Deviation Analysis

Year To Date Report P&L Deviation	A Actual	B Budget	C Deviation (B–A)	D % Deviation (C/B x 100)
Sales Revenue				
Products				
Other				
Returns & Allowances				
Net Revenue				
Cost Of Goods				
Beginning Merchandise Inventory				
Net Purchases Of Merchandise				
Ending Merchandise Inventory				
Total COGS				
Gross Margin				
Operating Expenses				
Salaries, etc. (F)				
Rent & Utilities (F)				
Insurance (F)				

Marketing & Advertising (F/V)				
Travel (V)				
Meals & Entertainment (V)				
Professional Fees (F)				
Telephone (F/V)				
Equipment Leases (F)				
Repairs & Maintenance (F)				
Amortization & Depreciation (F)				
Miscellaneous (F)				
Total Operating Expenses				
EBIT				
Interest Expense (F)				
Pretax Profit (Loss)				
Federal Taxes				
State Taxes				
Net Profit (Loss)				

Variance Analysis

Variance analysis is a simple and effective tool that provides an easy format to compare your company's actual to its projected performance, both monthly and YTD. You should adopt a version of deviation to make your budgets effective.

Furthermore, it takes only a few seconds to spot variances, and in many cases you'll already understand why they appear. The unexpected and subtler variances may indicate that you're doing something very right (or wrong). They help you to latch onto opportunities and blunt threats before it's too late.

If you prepare an annual cash flow pro forma, the cash flow budget is the best way to control the movement of cash into and out of your business. Ideally you would use the P&L budget to foster profitability and the cash flow budget to ensure liquidity. Steady ongoing businesses can afford to focus on profitability, as their cash flows don't threaten their liquidity. Businesses undergoing change should stress liquidity rather than profitability.

Break-Even Analysis

Break-even analysis (B/E) comes in two flavors: P&L or cash flow. Either one will help in a large number of decisions: Should you buy or lease that piece of equipment? Should you hire that salesperson now or later? Will you be able to produce the required sales volume? The uses are limited only by your willingness to use B/E as a guide to decision-making.

B/E is no silver bullet. The basic idea that B/E is built on is that covering the nut, those fixed monthly expenses that have to be met no matter what level of sales you achieve, together with variable expenses, establishes a base sales level at which you neither make or lose money. Schematically, it develops like this:

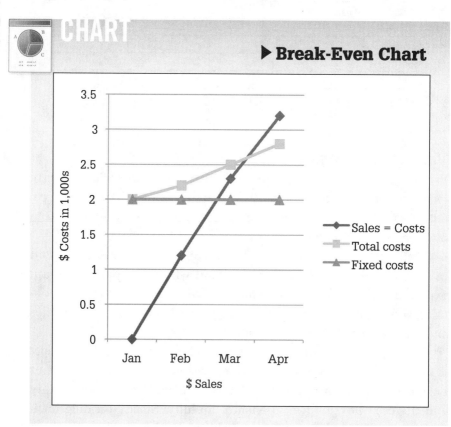

▶ **Break-Even Chart**

Costs in dollars are plotted on the vertical axis, sales in dollars on the horizontal axis. The diagonal line is where sales exactly equal costs.

Fixed costs are the same no matter what the sales level is so a horizontal line parallel to the sales axis represents them. The point where the Fixed Cost and Sales = Cost lines intersect would be the break-even point for a business with no variable costs. Such a business might exist, perhaps on another planet, or in another economy. Variable costs go up or down with sales levels.

The heavy diagonal arrow shows variable costs schematically. If fixed costs were $0, the diagonal would begin at the intersection of the Sales = Cost axes. Since there are fixed costs in most businesses, we simply start the variable cost line at the intersection of $0 sales and whatever the fixed costs happen to be. This generates the Total costs line.

The break-even point is the intersection of the Total cost and Sales = Cost lines. At this point, sales will generate exactly the revenue needed to cover all costs.

This can be expressed mathematically. The formulas are:

▶ Break-Even Equations

Cash Break-Even	=	Fixed Costs/ (1 – [Variable Costs/Sales])
P&L Break-Even	=	Fixed Expenses/ (1 – [Variable Expenses/Sales])

The beauty of break-even analysis is that given the basic formulas you can express your business' break-even point in terms of units sold, numbers of customers, or similar familiar quantities. One example is a small restaurant whose owner figured his break-even in terms of bowls of soup sold per day. He discovered that his restaurant couldn't serve enough customers during peak periods to come close to break-even so he changed his marketing strategy to a highly profitable luncheon take-out and delivery operation. Financial analysis and control can lead to unexpectedly profound results.

Break-even analysis proceeds simply. Fixed expenses or costs are (relatively) independent of sales. Keep in mind that they are fixed only within limits, because if sales grow dramatically, the fixed costs

T MORE

▶ **Some Useful Conversions**

(B-E = Break-Even)

Annual B-E/12	= Monthly sales needed
	= Monthly B-E
Monthly B-E/4.3	= Weekly sales needed
	= Weekly B-E
Weekly B-E/Work Days	= Daily sales needed
	= Daily B-E
Daily B-E/Hours Worked	= Average hourly sales needed
Average B-E/Average Price	= Units that have to be sold per hour
Monthly B-E/Average Price	= Units that have to be sold per month
Daily B-E/Average Price	= Units that have to be sold per day (for example bowls of soup)

will be forced to change too, albeit erratically, in discontinuous steps rather than a smooth, controllable curve. If you move to larger quarters, bang! Rent moves from $2,000/month to $5,000/month. Personnel costs hurtle upward. New equipment and more vehicles are necessary.

But with that warning in mind, many expenses can be treated as if they were fixed. Most of these are clear: rent, loan payments, payroll. A few seem a bit murky: Is the telephone fixed or variable? To be conservative, allocate any questionable item to fixed. A more aggressive approach is to split the cost, assigning a portion to each. Happily, these items in the middle are not only few in number, they also tend to be small in amount.

Should you use a cash flow or P&L break-even? Some prefer to use the P&L B/E and add profit goals to the fixed expenses. If your business is in a start-up or transitional mode, use a cash flow break-even. You should always look at the cash flow break-even first, paying special attention to operating needs. The break-even helps answer the questions: Is it necessary? Can we do without it? Why do we need it? How can we pay for it? Questions that come up whenever a capital investment is contemplated.

- ▶ **Start-ups and businesses in transition:** Use cash flow B/E.
- ▶ **Ongoing businesses:** Use P&L B/E.
- ▶ **Fast-growth businesses:** Use both cash flow and P&L B/E.

As an example, look at the one-year P&L projection on page 176. Follow the same process for your business, if you will be using a P&L B/E.

Step 1:   Allocate Expenses to Fixed or Variable

Cost of goods sold is variable. Marketing and advertising is F/V, but to be conservative, add this to Fixed. Small businesses benefit from conservative financial management.

Net Revenue	1,795
COGS	1,076
Gross Margin	718
Fixed Expenses	
Salaries	324
Rent & Utilities	30
Insurance	14
Marketing & Advertising	48
Professional Fees	2
Telephone	7
Equipment Leases	5
Repairs & Maintenance	2
Amortization & Depreciation	24
Miscellaneous	2
Interest	18
Total Fixed Expenses	**476**
Variable Expenses	
COGS	1,076
Travel	7
Meals & Entertainment	4
Total Variable Expenses	**1,087**

Using historical patterns rather than your projected or forecast figures is dangerous unless you feel confident that next year will be very much the same as last. Use forecasts to link your plans and goals more closely to operating realities. This yields better standards.

Step 2:   Add the Totals and Do the Arithmetic

P&L Break-even   =   Fixed Expenses/
                             (1–(Variable Expenses/Sales))

Fixed expenses   = $476,000
Variable expenses = $1,087,000
Sales   = $1,795,000

                         = $476,000/(1–(120,90,000/1,795,000))
                         = $475,000/(1–67)
                         = $1,439,000

Compare this break-even based on a P&L to the Cash flow B/E derived from the cash flow pro forma.

Cash From Operations	1,795
COGS	1,076
Gross Margin	718
Fixed Costs (Disbursements)	
Salaries	327
Rent & Utilities	30
Insurance	14
Marketing & Advertising	48
Professional Fees	2
Telephone	7
Equipment Leases	5
Repairs & Maintenance	2
Miscellaneous	2
Interest	18
Total Fixed Costs	455
Variable Costs	
COGS	1,200
Travel	7
Meals & Entertainment	4
Total Variable Costs	**1,211**

Cash Break-Even   =   Fixed Costs/(1–(Variable Costs/Sales))

Fixed Costs   = $455
(Disbursements)

Variable Costs (Disbursements)	=	$1,211
Cash Inflows (from Sales)	=	$1,795

$$= \$455/(1-(\$1,211/\$1,795))$$
$$= \$455/(1-67)$$
$$= \$455/0.33$$
$$= \$1,378$$

If your business is on the edge, use the cash flow version to monitor progress. Survival is your primary goal. If undergoing rapid change, use both methods.

How might you use these figures? Here are a few ways:

1. **Number of units per year.** Assume the average price per unit is $10. You have to sell nearly 50,000 units to make profit goals, 44,000 to break even on cash. What if you raised the price to an average $12/unit? Your cash B/E drops to 36,000 units, while your Profit B/E drops to 40,000 units. Now this may or may not be achievable. Price points are sensitive issues and a rise in price might seriously hurt sales. No business decision is made in a vacuum, but B/E gives you some roughly accurate numbers to help inform your pricing decisions.

2. **Note that these are only roughly accurate.** Lower unit sales translate into somewhat lowered production costs (COGS), which would make B/E more attainable. Yet again: If you err, let it be in the cautious direction. The sense of accuracy gained by re-juggling the P&L and cash flow isn't worth the effort. Financial management doesn't require such fine-tuning and, indeed, is somewhat scornful of the effort. Better to use a simple tool than a complicated one you let rust in its box.

3. **Profit B/E of 50,000 units equals approximately 1,000 units a week or 4,300 units per month.** How will these sales be gained? Or given the patterns of historical sales should you look to longer periods as an ongoing measure? A rolling

three-month average? Perhaps. Sales are made one by one. If the average sale is 10 units, then you need 5,000 sales, or 430 per month. These ruminations help set strategies and monitor progress. These figures can be worked backward up the sales funnel and expressed in such terms as numbers of calls, prospecting and other, and letters and marketing concentrations. Never forget that sales drive everything. The numbers are useful in getting sales and in improving the selling process.

4. **What happens if you add a salesperson at a cost of $75,000 plus expenses of $15,000 and a 6 percent sales commission?** How many sales dollars must she generate to pay for herself—let alone generate a profit—and is it likely that she'll make those sales? The math is simple:

> **Fixed Cost increase = $75,000 + 15,000 = $90,000**
> = $90,000/(1–(0.33 +0.6))
> = $90,000/0.6
> = $150,000

This approximation is close enough to help you make a rational decision. Are additional sales of $150,000 achievable? Perhaps. It depends on the context. It represents 15,000 units for a year, or an average of 1,250 units per month. For a beginner, is this realistic? The answer depends on how other salespeople have initially performed, how strong the territory, competition, and the economy are, and the experience and training of the individual.

An important line of thought proceeds from looking at the composition of your costs:

1. **Service industries typically have low fixed costs and medium variable costs, resulting in a low break-even point.** Profits go up with sales once the break-even is reached.
2. **Manufacturers usually have high fixed costs and low variable costs.** Once break-even is finally reached, small sales increases lead to large profit increases.

3. **Construction firms have low fixed costs and high variable costs, leading to a high break-even point.** Large sales increases lead to relatively small increases in profit, which can cause cash problems, though if the numbers are large enough, profits can be immense.

You should know the cost pattern of your business. If you are heavy with fixed costs, first prune those costs as much as possible and then drive the revenues. If fixed costs are relatively low but variable costs are high, look for economies on the variable costs first, then drive revenue. This assumes that these changes are made in the context of your more general business plans. Recognition of your cost patterns can help you decide whether cost cutting or pushing for higher revenues would be more appropriate for your firm. Usually it will turn out to be a combination of efforts, on both the cost reduction and revenue improvement sides, but you benefit from knowing which strategy will yield the best returns.

Degree of Operating Leverage

Degree of operating leverage (DOL) is a closely related tool. *DOL* uses variable costs, accounts receivable, accounts payable, inventory, and cash to determine what sales increase is needed to generate a dollar of cash.

Most people, when confronted by a cash squeeze, think they can quickly generate sales to pull through enough cash fast enough to relieve the pressure. While this may work (and in some ways must be the long-term solution), two forces make it unlikely. The first is the business truism that sales never turn to cash as fast as you hope they will. It takes time for your customers to pay, especially if you offer credit or extend payment terms. It takes time to process the invoice, time for the post office to move an envelope across town, time to cut the check once the customer receives the invoice, and time for the check to be mailed back to your office.

The other force is DOL (see the chart on the next page). As sales rise, so do a host of related costs. You need more inventory and perhaps more variable labor to push orders through. The net effect is that you will raise less money over a longer time than you plan.

In other words, a sales increase of $4.38 results in a cash increase of

KEY INFO

▶ The DOL Formula

$$DOL = \frac{S}{(S - V - (CE + A/R + I - A/P)\,(I - T))}$$

S   = Total Sales
V   = Variable Costs
CE = Cash and Equivalent
A/R = Accounts Receivable
I   = Inventory
A/P = Accounts Payable
T   = Income Tax Rate

This example uses figures from Aardvark's projected balance sheet and the cash flow pro forma.

$$DOL = \frac{\$1{,}795}{(\$1{,}795 - \$1{,}211 - (\$115 + \$165 + \$265 - \$105)\,(1 - 0.10))}$$

$$= \frac{\$1{,}795}{\$409} = \$4.38$$

$1. Just how long it will take to generate this hypothetical $1 is another matter. An average retail store needs a sales increase of more than $5 to generate a single solitary $1 of cash. Your business's DOL will naturally depend on your business's distribution of costs and balance sheet.

Note that high cash, accounts receivable, and inventory figures will increase your DOL, while higher accounts payable will tend to decrease your DOL. This means that if you can safely run your business with lean cash and inventory, and keep accounts receivable low by diligent collection efforts, your sales will turn to cash more rapidly. Reducing accounts payable, on the other hand, may be a poor strategy. Pay on time and take discounts, but don't prepay.

The implications of DOL vary from one business to another, but the underlying principle is the same. A dollar increase in sales is a slower route to generating cash than careful management of accounts receivable and accounts payable.

26

Controlling Inventory and Receivables

Your two largest current assets are receivables and inventory. However, unless they are managed with cash flow in mind, they can become hidden cash drains.

To manage these assets properly, you must know:

- ▶ The ages of your receivables and inventory
- ▶ The turns of your receivables and inventory
- ▶ The concentration of your receivables (how many customers, what dollar amount of receivables they represent, what products the receivables cover)
- ▶ The concentration of your inventory by product lines

You must also know what effects your credit and collection policies have on your working capital and cash flow. Small business owners all too often mistake sales for profits. They extend more and more credit, practice lax collection policies, and end up providing interest-free loans to their customers in the name of increasing sales. Many business owners have found that their largest accounts actually cost them money because of slow payment.

No small business owner can afford to provide interest-free loans to his or her biggest customers, but unless you take the time to analyze the payment behavior of your slow-paying accounts, you may not know what's eating up your cash flow.

This isn't to say don't increase credit sales. The aim is profitability and positive cash flow, not sales increases. If the sales don't translate into bottom-line profits, then you're buying trouble as fast as you are buying sales.

 TABLE

▶ Aardvark, Inc.

Balance Sheet Comparison

	12/31/10	12/31/11
Current Assets		
Cash	$112,050	$97,950
Accounts Receivable	$140,400	$150,000
Inventory	$225,450	$253,500
Prepaid Expenses	$20,550	$28,800
Current Assets Total	**$498,450**	**$530,250**
Fixed Assets		
Property, Plant, and Equipment	$403,500	$495,000
Accumulated Depreciation	−$103,950	−$127,500
Cost Less Depreciation	$299,550	$367,500
Intangible Assets	$150,000	$167,250
Fixed assets total	**$449,550**	**$534,750**
Total assets	**$948,000**	**$1,065,000**
Liabilities		
Accounts Payable	$80,250	$99,600
Accrued Expenses Payable	$31,050	$45,450
Income Tax Payable	$2,460	$4,950
Short-Term Notes Payable	$90,000	$93,750

Total Current Liabilities	**$203,760**	**$243,750**
Long-Term Liabilities		
Notes Payable	$20,000	$21,250
Notes Payable (Long-Term)	$40,000	$30,000
Bank Loans Payable	$0	$0
Deferred Taxes	$50,000	$45,000
Other Loans Payable	$0	$0
Other Long-Term Liabilities	$0	$0
Total Long-Term Liabilities	**$110,000**	**$96,250**
Total Liabilities	**$313,760**	**$340,000**
Net Worth		
Retained Earnings	$394,240	$485,000
Invested Capital	$240,000	$240,000
Total Net Worth	$634,240	$725,000
Total Liabilities & Net Worth	**$948,000**	**$1,065,000**

P&L, 1/1/11—12/31/11

Sales Revenue		$1,560,000
COGS		$1,014,000
Gross Margin		$546,000
SG&A		$374,400
Depreciation		$23,550
Earnings Before Interest and Income Tax		$148,050
Interest Expense		$16,350
EBIT		$131,700
Income tax		$52,440
Net Income		**$79,260**

Receivables Management

Begin by examining the age of your receivables every week. This helps you spot the slow-paying accounts early, so you can begin collection efforts as soon as possible.

Separate invoices into current, 30 days old, 60 days, 90 days, and over. This is called "aging the receivables." You want to set up your aging schedule on the credit terms you offer—current, 10-day, and so on (if you offer 10-day terms). The main idea is to spot those customers who pay within term (so you can find more of them) and those who don't (so you can reeducate or avoid them in the future).

Then, figure out your collection period: Divide annual credit sales (from your historical figures or from projections) by 360 to find the average daily credit sale. Next, divide your current outstanding receivables total by the average daily credit sale figure. This gives you your current receivables collection period.

Don't forget to consider seasonality. If sales tend to cluster, your accounts receivable will peak at the time of sales and distort the collection picture. Department stores, for example, have huge receivables at the beginning of the year, much smaller receivables in the late spring.

A rule of thumb: if your collection period is more than one third greater than your credit terms (for example, 40 days if your terms are Net 30), you have a cash cycle or collection problem that needs your immediate attention.

Follow these five steps in receivables management:

1. **Age your receivables.**
2. **Calculate your collection period.** Use the rule of thumb to check for problems.
3. **Identify and vigorously pursue the slow-paying customers.**
4. **Identify and try to find more fast-paying or term-paying accounts.**
5. **Measure the impact of your credit and collection policies on your cash flow by playing "what-if" with your projections.** Perhaps changing your terms could improve cash flow and profits.

▶ Collection Period

Here is the formula to determine the length of Aardvark's collection period:

The first number to determine is the average daily credit sale. This is reached by dividing total annual credit sales by 360. In Aardvark's case, 85 percent of sales are made on credit.

Yearly sales: 1,560,000
Credit sales: 1,326,000

The average daily credit sale is:
$1,326,000/360 = $3,683

Once the average daily credit sale is determined, divide it into the current outstanding receivables to find the collection period. As of 12/31/11, Aardvark's accounts receivables figure is $150,000:

$150,000/$3,683 = 40.7 days

The result is that Aardvark is maintaining a 40.7-day collection period. This doesn't look bad since their terms are Net 30 but it is definitely an area that needs to be corrected. If their terms had been Net 10, this would have been well beyond acceptable limits. The higher this collection period climbs, the more Aardvark will find itself getting out of the retail business and into the banking business.

Inventory Management

Carrying costs of inventory run as high as 30 percent of average inventory, a substantial drain on working capital. Add the costs of insurance, storage, spoilage, pilferage, handling, and maintenance to the cost of inventory loans. It adds up fast.

It's hard to determine the right amounts of inventory to carry. The balance is between stock outs and unnecessary expenses, compounded by supplier delivery and reorder times. Some of the factors that your inventory policies should reflect (in addition to the marketing and sales factors, which are dominant): Inventory or stock turn: How often do you turn (sell) your inventory? How does that compare with other businesses in your industry?

KEY INFO

▶ Inventory Turnover

You calculate your inventory turnover as follows:

**Average inventory =
(Beginning inventory + Ending inventory)/2**

Aardvark's average inventory:
**= (225,450 + 253,500)/2
= 239,475**

Cost of goods sold/Average inventory (in $) = Inventory turnover. For Aardvark this is:

1,014,000/239,475 = 4.2

Thus, Aardvark turns its inventory 4.2 times a year.

MORE

▶ Inventory Management Tips

▶ You have to keep track of reorder times. The difference between a 10-day reorder time and a 210-day reorder is enormous, and will affect the level of reserve inventory you carry.

▶ Who are your suppliers? Where are they located? Delivery times are important.

▶ What trade terms do your suppliers give you? Taking a 2 percent discount on terms of 2/10, Net 30 is equivalent to earning a 72 percent annual yield. That's considerably more than the interest your bank charges, and has implications for your ordering and inventory policies.

27

Digression on Credit and Collections

The cost of extending credit is a good example of the hidden costs that devour working capital. Most small business owners aren't credit experts. They grant credit because other businesses do, and often fail to understand what the impact on profits and cash flow will be. Few small businesses have explicit credit and collection policies, so they lose twice: granting the credit, and then having to collect funds later. If you establish credit and collection policies appropriate to your business, you will increase profits, the quality of your current assets, and the speed of your cash flow.

Your trade association will have reams of information about normal credit practices for your industry. These are good guides but you may be able to improve on trade figures. Check with your banker, accountant, or other qualified professional. Ask friendly competitors at trade shows—those competitors who aren't in your trading area.

Credit and collection policies are difficult to establish because they are tied so closely to cash flow and sales. Easier credit terms tend to

T

▶ Credit and Debit Cards

Investigate the use of credit and debit cards. These cost little in return for the headaches they can save you. Consider the costs in direct bad debt losses as well as in the time, effort, and attention slow-pay accounts cost you. Then add the costs of capital tied up in receivables to the interest you pay to carry those receivables. Are credit and debit cards worth it? Probably—but you can get a dollars-and-cents answer from your accountant.

boost sales, though often at the cost of lower profits if the sales don't turn to cash on time. Tighter credit requirements, on the other hand, result in lowered sales, often at the cost of additional profits from those fringe accounts that turn out to be good though slow payers.

Set Credit Objectives

Why extend credit? Look to your business goals. Credit objectives should be derived from your wider business objectives. If you're entering a new market, your credit policies might reflect the importance of acquiring new customers even if they have shaky credit. If for some reason you want to limit the number of customers, you would impose more stringent terms. Once again, the context drives your decisions.

You have to be clear on the objectives your credit policies are intended to achieve.

Ask yourself the following questions:

- ▶ **Why should we extend credit?**
- ▶ **What do we hope to achieve by extending credit (stated in terms of additional sales, dollars of added profit, number of customers)?**
- ▶ **What has our credit policy achieved in the past?**
- ▶ **What would we ideally achieve by changing our credit policies?**
- ▶ **What changes in credit policies would lead to these desired goals?**
- ▶ **The more precise you can make the objectives the better. How many dollars of increased sales or profits? When? How many customers would that represent?**

Chapter 27

Determine the Credit Capacity of Your Business

The basic question is: Can I afford to extend these credits? To get a rough fix, look at your accounts receivables and compare the total with the amount of short-term debt you carry. If you extend more credit than your business can afford, your short-term debt will be high relative to the current level of receivables. Look to industry and trade averages to compare performance to your competition. Ask your banker and accountant for advice. Borrowing from a bank to support slow-paying customers is a sure route to disaster unless your margins (and reserves for bad debt) are high and you know the costs and accept them as part of doing business.

Short-term debt may be high for other reasons (inventory or bridge financing, for examples). But if you have to constantly borrow against your receivables, then you'd better sit down with your banker and overhaul your credit and collection policies.

The amount of credit you can extend is directly tied to your cash flow. Ask: What will the impact of delayed receipt of payables do to our ability to pay our own bills? Good cash flow lets you extend credit. If it is a constant struggle to meet fixed payments, then vigorously pursue any way you can accelerate cash flow (that includes turning accounts receivable into cash faster). Tighter credit restrictions will ordinarily improve cash flow at the cost of reduced sales and profits.

Establish and Follow Credit-Checking Procedures

The best time to improve collection results is before any credit is granted. To safely extend credit you must know your customers. Some of the most important information will come from your bank. Your bank will have a standard credit information form. Providing credit information is a normal bank service for its business depositors.

Credit managers divide customers and prospects in four groups: prime customers who provide full operating profits by paying within terms or take discounts; good, who provide 70 to 80 percent of operating profit; average, who provide 50 percent of operating profit; and others who expose you to late payments and bad debt losses. Your aim is to garner as many prime and good customers as possible. If you check credit in advance you can identify these desirable groups. Businesses, like people, tend to follow behavior patterns.

Some information to gather before granting credit:

▶ **Net worth of customer**
▶ **Credit history**
▶ **Number of employees**
▶ **Length of time in business**
▶ **Names of three or more vendors**
▶ **Names and credit history of principals**

KEY INFO

▶ **Credit Checklist**

Customer Name:
Date:
1. **D&B Rating**

2. **Trade Reference 1**
   a. Talked to:
   b. Account open since
   c. Last sale
   d. Terms
   e. High credit
   f. Amount owing
   g. Amount past due
   h. Pays within
   i. Comments

3. **Trade Reference 2**
   a. Talked to:
   b. Account open since

   c. Last sale
   d. Terms
   e. High credit
   f. Amount owing
   g. Amount past due
   h. Pays within
   i. Comments

3. **Bank Reference:**
   a. Branch
   b. Officer's name
   c. Checking account since
   d. Average high balance
   e. Is it a satisfactory
      account?
   f. High credit
   g. Payment history
   h. Comments:

Control Accounts Receivable by Carefully Allocating Credit

Your accountant will help you determine what kind of profit you can expect from selling on credit to each of the various categories (prime, good, average, or other). Some businesses seek out poor credit risks. You've probably seen television commercials that specifically ask, "Do you have poor credit?" or saying, "Good people with poor credit deserve cars, too!" Such customers cannot get credit from normal sources so are willing to pay a higher price. It's your call as to whether the increased sales outweigh the credit risks, even if there will be significant delinquency and collection problems.

The basic information you need to manage your accounts receivable is gained by aging your receivables. This means listing them by due dates. For example: Current, 30 days, 60 days, and Over 60 days. If you extend 30-day terms and your customers pay in 60 days in spite of your best efforts, it's time to change your credit procedures. If they pay in 40 days, you are probably OK.

To determine the average collection period for credit sales:

Annual Credit Sales/365 = **Daily credit sales**
Collection period in days = **Accounts receivable/**
Daily credit sales

The collection period should be no more than one-third longer than your net selling terms.

Establish and Apply Collection Procedures

Your collection procedures should be firm, consistent, and courteous. Think of the Golden Rule. How would you like to be treated if for some reason beyond your control you couldn't pay a bill?

The convention is to send a reminder letter the day the account becomes overdue. Then make a phone call to the customer, identify the person responsible for paying the invoice, and ask politely but firmly for payment. This can be difficult if dealing with large organizations— they can "lose" invoices on a regular basis. Try to get a payment date and take clear notes for reference in the future.

Keep track of your customers' payment history. You may want to put some on COD, set up a partial repayment plan, or otherwise find a way to get your money while retaining the customer's good will. (Naturally, there will be some customers you won't want to keep.) Turn to collection agencies as a last resort. They can be more aggressive than you might want to be and are skilled at getting payments from apparent stones.

KEY INFO

▶ Collections

Use the form below for every collection call. It helps if you're forced into litigation.

Name:	Comments:
Telephone:	
Spoke to:	
Title:	
Subject:	Returned call:
	Follow-up:
Date:	
Time:	
Initials:	
No answer:	☐ Not available
Requested info:	☐ Requested proof of delivery
Order never received:	☐ Payment previously sent
Will send check:	☐ Merchandise returned
Duplicate billing:	☐ Payment being held

Monitor, Review, and Change Credit and Collection Policies as Needed

All policies need to be reviewed regularly. Business conditions change constantly. When monitoring and reviewing policies and procedures, ask yourself:

▶ **Are the credit objectives being met?**
▶ **Has the credit capacity of the business changed?**
▶ **Should the credit policies be changed again?**
▶ **Should you aim for more average and other customers?**
▶ **Have bad debt losses and delinquency rates decreased in dollars and numbers?**

Your credit and collection policies, properly established and applied, will help you increase profits. Making sure that you have the appropriate policies in place is a good investment of your time and effort.

Part Five

Using the Financials to Finance Your Business

How to Secure the Right Bank Financing at the Right Time for *Your* Business

28

Startup Financing: A Special Case

Startups are special. They are exciting, exhausting, potentially very profitable, and always very risky. Many startups fail. Many more never evolve beyond the bare survival stage. They lack capital, marketing expertise, access to economies of scale, and bank support. A few—a very few—prosper. Treat turnarounds as startups. They are just as risky. It takes as much (or more) effort to turn a slipping company around as it takes to start up a new one.

Startups demand business plans. Your startup business plan lets you model ideas, predict costs, and play "what-if" without risking your savings and time. The success of your startup is related to the amount and depth of research you put into your plan.

Your ability to discipline yourself to stick with the plan once it has been prepared is another factor. It doesn't matter what your venture is—retail, service, manufacturing, high or low tech. Stick-to-it-iveness plus a good plan make ventures succeed, while lack of perseverance and discipline scuttle even the best business idea (no matter how

▶ What Sets the Successes Apart From the Failures and the Walking Dead?

- ▶ They are carefully planned.
- ▶ They are well capitalized.
- ▶ They are niche players.
- ▶ They're not pioneers.
- ▶ They learn from their errors.
- ▶ They learn from their competitors.
- ▶ They're managed according to a method.
- ▶ They are client-(customer-)centered.

well capitalized). You hope to raise capital and secure credit on the strength of your business plan.

Three key points:

1. **Your business idea must be clear, concise, and communicable.**
2. **Your marketing plan must be carefully and patiently detailed and followed.**
3. **Your sales forecasts have to be accurate and demonstrable.**
4. **Armed with such a plan, your chances of establishing a successful business are good.**

Nobody wants to finance a startup except the entrepreneur and perhaps his or her immediate family and friends. Banks are not in the startup financing business. Bankers do lend to individuals even if they claim not to lend to startups. All credit sources look at your track record. By definition, startups don't have one, but you have a personal credit history that will be scrutinized closely.

It's hard to get trade credit for a startup. Would you lend money or extend credit to a brand new company you'd never heard of? Of course not. Then why would they?

In fact, few businesses want to do business with a startup. If your business will be selling to other businesses, you'll quickly discover that reliability and reputation are extremely important in business-to-business sales. Price, convenience, and service are swell, but take second place. This is true to a lesser extent in retail businesses.

Chapter 28

Inertia is the greatest human force. Even new professional services run a risk of failure. People are reluctant to switch from their current lawyer or accountant. Most people prefer the devil they know to the devil they don't.

You aren't your own boss in a startup. Your business is your boss. The business sets your hours, pay level, retirement, and other benefits. Everyone else is also your boss: Your customers, creditors, suppliers—even your employees pull your strings. The cheerful, naive notion of "being your own boss" is a Hollywood fantasy out of Horatio Alger.

Startups are the riskiest way to get into business. This has been proven so often it seems silly to bring it up again, but entrepreneurs fortunately don't know any better. Nor do corporate dropouts. Clawing out a niche in the competitive marketplace takes a lot of stamina, planning, capital, and luck.

Startups are fun and worth pursuing if you have the stomach and stamina. Even if your first venture flops, you can learn from it. Sure, a franchise or an acquisition is safer and for most business ventures far more profitable. But in a startup you imprint your own ideas and values on an organization, set your working conditions (to a degree), and create a structure that's incredibly rewarding if it succeeds. If you aren't an optimist, or if you need the security of a regular paycheck, don't try a startup.

Startup Financing

You have to fully invest in your startup. If you don't, any investor is sure to ask, "If you won't take a chance on this, why should I?" If you're not willing to take the maximum amount of risk your circumstances will allow, then outsiders won't be willing to take even a small risk.

Think of the old story about a plate of ham and eggs. The chicken makes a *contribution* but the pig makes a *commitment.* When starting a new business, the investor is the chicken. The entrepreneur must take the other role.

You may have more to invest than you think.

Sell Assets

If you own things, you can sell them. It's that simple. Jewelry, rugs, pool tables, boats, time-shares, and vacation homes—the list goes on.

Most people's largest assets are their homes and cars. Here is what you can do with cars.

If you drive a nice, late-model car, you can sell it and lease a cheap one without a down payment. This might net you $15,000 to $20,000 and leave you with a small monthly lease payment.

Even if you lease your car, a variation on this theme applies. Suppose you lease a brand-new sport utility vehicle for $449 per month. Get rid of it, and lease an economy car for $125 per month. Granted, the savings of $320 each month isn't much to start a business on. However, this new monthly cash flow should allow you to secure a personal loan. With that much, you may be able to borrow as much as $12,000.

Borrow Against Your Home

This is the oldest trick in the book. It's also one of the best because you can exert almost total control over the process. Here's how it works: Say you need $50,000, your home is worth $250,000, and you owe the bank $100,000 on your mortgage. You can borrow against the equity, which in this case is $150,000.

Most banks and mortgage companies will lend up to 80 percent of the equity in your home. So in the hypothetical example, the $150,000 of equity would allow you (the homeowner/entrepreneur) to borrow up to $120,000.

Of course, once the loan kicks in, you'll have monthly payments. If you're starting a new business, it's a wise idea to set aside some of the proceeds from the home equity loan to help make these payments until the business can pay you a steady salary.

Another way to get money out of your home but maintain a lower monthly payment is to refinance the mortgage with a new one.

Using the above hypothetical example, rather than borrowing against the equity, you would get a new thirty-year mortgage for $150,000 and with the proceeds pay off the $100,000 mortgage. The difference, $50,000, can be used for any purpose you want, including investing in a new business.

The refinancing option is less expensive because payments on the $50,000 are spread across thirty years instead of perhaps ten years for a home equity loan. In the long run, however, the lower payments will prove to be more expensive, since the borrower is paying interest on the outstanding balance for perhaps as long as thirty years. With a shorter loan, you will pay significantly less interest. But can you afford the higher monthly payments?

Borrow Against Insurance Policies

If you want to know where all your money goes, look at your insurance payments. Each month, you likely pay for health insurance, life insurance, disability insurance, auto insurance, and homeowner's insurance.

You can only borrow against whole life policies. Most have some cash value after three years. Simply write your agent or insurance company, saying you want a policy loan. Most companies will lend up to 90 percent of the cash value, and your policy will stay intact as long as you keep paying the premiums as they come due. However, if you die with a policy loan outstanding, the benefits might be diminished, although that varies by policy. The good news is that loans against your insurance policy are fairly reasonable, since the rates charged are tied to the key money market rate.

Friends and Family

They believe in you the most. Therefore, they should be one of the first outside sources of capital you tap.

Friends and family present a formidable source of capital. The typical friend or family investor is male, has been successful in his own business, and wants to invest because he wishes someone had done it for him, according to Kirk Neiswander, senior vice president of Enterprise Development Inc., a nonprofit subsidiary of Case Western Reserve University's Weatherhead School of Management. "They are not reckless investors, and they have shallow pockets," he says. "They will invest once but not a second or a third time and generally in an industry they know that is close to home. Typically, friends and family will invest up to $100,000."

However, investments with friends and family can turn out poorly when things don't go as planned. The situation can be even worse than with professional investors because friends and family react to bad news as much with emotion as with logic. Take the following steps to protect everyone involved:

1. **Get an agreement in writing, which will eliminate all conversations that start with, "You never said that."**

2. **Emphasize debt (loans) rather than equity (ownership).** You don't want friends and family in your company forever. Before you know it, they'll start telling you how to run the place, and long-buried emotions will emerge. Make it a loan, and pay it back as fast as you can. This also protects the lender against imputed income on the loan, which can result in an unexpected tax to the lender.

3. **Put some cash flow on their investment.** If your sister says, "Here's $50,000—try not to lose it, and pay it back as soon as you can," that's great. Document the loan. Consider paying some nominal interest at regular intervals so that you and she both have a reality check. And it's better to pay it quarterly than monthly. That way, when things are teetering, your lender won't immediately know it.

Borrow Against Your Investments

Margin loans are cheap and easy if the market is rising, but if the market is falling (remember 2008–2010), they can be disastrous. Margin loans are easy because any brokerage firm with which you have an account will lend you money against the value of your holdings. For instance, you can borrow up to 90 percent of the value of federal government bills, bonds, and notes. For municipal bonds the advance rate is 75 percent, for government agencies it's 65 percent, and for stocks and mutual funds it's 50 percent. Margin loans are cheap because the underlying collateral is accessible (it's in your account) and it's liquid (it can be sold and quickly turned into cash).

Assuming you have $50,000 worth of blue-chip stocks in your portfolio, and you've applied for margin privileges, one phone call to your broker will get you $25,000. It's that easy.

Margin loans are not for everyone. In fact, they might even be a last resort. But if you're at that point, then you have to do what you have to do.

Do you have a job and a 401(k)? If you start your business part-time while keeping your full-time job, consider borrowing against your employer's 401(k) retirement plan. It's common for such plans to let you borrow a percentage of your money that doesn't exceed $50,000. The interest rate is usually comparable to the bank prime rate, with a specified repayment schedule. The downside of borrowing from your

401(k) is that if you lose your job, the loan must be repaid immediately. To see if this is an option, consult your plan's documentation.

You may also want to consider using the funds in your IRA. Within the laws governing IRAs, you can actually withdraw money from an IRA as long as you replace it within sixty days. This is not a loan, so you don't pay interest; rather, this is a withdrawal that you are allowed to keep for sixty days. A highly organized person could possibly juggle funds among several IRAs. But if you're one day late—for any reason—you'll be hit with a 10 percent premature withdrawal fee, and the money you haven't returned will become taxable.

Credit Cards

They are not terribly creative, but credit cards are quick and easy. In a perverse way, they are also cheap. That is, a minimum payment of $50 per month can hold down a whole lot of debt. Of course, if you only make the minimum payment, your balance will continue to grow, and if the business fails, you'll have to pay the piper. But if things go well and the business pays off the balances without missing a beat, then you can look back at your early credit card financing with a nostalgic fondness and perhaps a twinge of longing for simpler days.

▶ A Piece of the Pie

The SBA's 8(a) Program is a small business set-aside that gives socially and economically disadvantaged entrepreneurs access to government contracts and provides management and technical assistance to help them develop their businesses. The 8(a) Program is a starter program for qualified businesses, which must leave the "nest" after nine years.

Entrepreneurs who participate in the 8(a) Program are eligible to apply for assistance under the 7(a) Loan Guaranty and Prequalification Loan programs. Although the 8(a) Program was once limited to minorities, recent regulatory changes allow women-, disabled- and veteran-owned firms to participate, in addition to African Americans, Hispanic Americans, Native Americans, and Asian-Pacific Americans.

T

▶ Meet Me in the Middle

The SBA's unique Prequalification Loan Program was designed to help business owners who are traditionally underserved by the lending community, including armed services veterans, minorities, women, and the disabled. Working with the aid of private intermediary organizations chosen by the SBA, eligible entrepreneurs prepare a business plan and complete a loan application. The intermediary submits the application to the SBA. If it's approved, the SBA issues the borrower a prequalification letter, which is taken, along with a loan package, to a commercial lender. The idea is that with the SBA's guarantee already in place, the bank is more likely to approve the loan. Through the program, qualified borrowers can apply for loans of up to $250,000.

29

Determine How Much You Need

O ne of the most dangerous errors small business owners make is to begin with a sum of dollars in mind as a borrowing target. The better way is to identify the business needs first and then consider the timing and duration of those needs. After this has been determined, you can turn to the question of how much you need.

For a startup, for example, you could list the capital assets you will need. Included in this list could be store fixtures, startup costs of equipment leases and rent deposits, operating equipment, and so forth. The fixed assets, those assets necessary to run the business, are the capital assets. Picture your business: What are the physical items that will be listed in dollar terms on your balance sheet? (Intangibles such as copyrights and patents are another matter.)

Suppose you have a going business. You have an ongoing need for a place to do business and the capital (fixed) assets. Then you need inventory to sell or materials to produce products—current assets. You need cash to pay employees and suppliers, purchase insurance, pay taxes... an endless list.

The key to all debt financing is to tie debt life to asset life. If the need is short-term or seasonal, pay off the loan as soon as possible or seasonally. If the need is permanent you should think about investing permanent capital.

KEY INFO

▶ Tie Debt Life to Asset Life

Purpose of Loan	Asset Life	Length of Loan	Source of Repayment
Equipment	1 to 3 years	1 to 3 years	Operating Profit
Equipment	4 to 8 years	4 years	Operating Profit
Working capital	NA	1 to 3 years	Operating Profit
Inventory	NA	One inventory turn	Sale of inventory
A/R (Secured)	Less than 1 year	< 1 year	Collection of A/R
Fixed asset purchase	8 or more years	8 to 15 years	Operating Profit

Term Loans

Bank term loans are often short-term, but because they are renewed over and over, they become longer-term loans, sometimes called "evergreens." Bankers prefer self-liquidating loans where the use of the loan money ensures an automatic repayment scheme. Most term loans have fixed interest rates and a set maturity date. Term loans may be paid monthly, quarterly, or annually. Some may have a balloon payment at the end of the term of the loan.

There are two types of term loans. The first is the intermediate term loan that usually has a maturity of one to three years. It is often used to finance working capital needs. Working capital refers to the daily operating funds that small business owners need to run their businesses.

Intermediate term loans can also be used to finance assets, such as machinery, that have a life of around one to three years, such as computer equipment or other small machinery or equipment. Repayment of the intermediate term loan is usually tied to the life of the equipment or the time for which you need the working capital.

Intermediate term loan agreements often have restrictive covenants put in place by the bank. *Restrictive covenants* restrict management operations during the life of the loan. They ensure that management will repay the loan before paying bonuses, dividends, and other optional payments.

Then there are long-term bank loans, the second type of term loan. Banks seldom provide long-term financing to small businesses. When they do, it's usually for the purchase of real estate or a large business facility. The bank will only lend 65 to 80 percent of the value of the asset the business is buying and the asset serves as collateral for the loan.

Loan Amounts

Now to the amounts sought. One way to control purchases or investments is to use a three-column approach similar to the one used in making the sales forecast. For every contemplated purchase or investment, try to put a dollar figure onto it that reflects an unlimited budget, a survival budget, and the most likely budget—one somewhere in between posh and penury. Don't forget to ask: Do we really need this? Really?

Step 1: Look at Your Capital Asset Costs

Purpose	Unlimited Budget	Most Likely Budget	Survival Budget
Buy computers	25,000	12,000	5,000
Furniture & fixtures	125,000	48,000	12,000

Pay for capital investments from invested capital, secondarily from the proceeds of long-term loans. Short-term needs should be covered by short-term debt, intermediate-term needs by intermediate-term loans.

Step 2: Look for Negative Cash Flow

The deepest negative cash flow is found by pushing the cash flow pro forma out far enough to be sure you'll have adequate operating positive cash flow to carry on normal business operations. This is especially important if you're in a period of fast growth or transition. Look for the cumulative cash flow total, the worst one during the period projected. Then double it to arrive at a range of required new capital.

Step 3: The Safety Margin

This is an added cushion, usually secured by invested capital, to let you sleep at night. Ask your accountant what a normal cushion might be for a business such as yours.

Step 4:   Add the Totals From Steps 1, 2, and 3

This gives you a rough idea of the total amount of debt and equity you need. If anything, it will call for more capital than is absolutely necessary.

Step 5:   Other Financing Purposes Than Capital Assets

Keep the battle cry "Do we really need this? Really?" in mind. It's good business to separate wants from needs. Then apply the three-column approach to get a likely figure for each need. If the need stands up and the dollar cost isn't out of reach, then you're in a position to know (not guess) how much money you need to raise.

30

Credit, Capital, or a Mix?

The key questions are whether to pursue debt money or invested capital, and in what proportion. Too much debt is dangerous. So is too much capital.

Whether the need is for debt or capital, you have to know the costs. One reason for the repeated warning against carrying too much debt is that the cost of that money, the interest and principal repayment, may equal or exceed the return you can earn after expenses on that money. This is a fine way to slowly go broke—almost painless—until suddenly there's no working capital and no credit.

High Debt-to-Net Worth ratios, high leverage, can show spectacular returns on invested capital. But if things don't work out—and they seldom do—then the loss figures are even more spectacular and net worth can vanish overnight. For a scary example on a macroeconomic level, an over-leveraged America lost $14 trillion dollars in the 2008–2010 recession due largely to the collapse of the housing market and the concomitant blow to the entire financial industry.

Too little capital will surface as negative net worth. The only remedy for negative net worth is new capital investment. In most cases financing sources are understandably leery of lending into a negative net worth situation. Would you invest in a company whose management lacked the basic foresight to properly capitalize the business? And then ran it at a loss to boot? Of course not. Yet that is exactly what many borrowers expect lenders to do.

Figure the cost. If you usually net 8 percent on gross sales, and debt costs your company 12 to 15 percent, then that cost must be justified in increased sales, increased efficiencies, greater profits, or all three. Otherwise, it becomes an added burden.

There are several ways to judge the "right" amount of debt. In retail, for example, the Sales-to-Net Worth ratio is useful. If your Sales/Net Worth ratio is consistently higher than trade averages, you are overtrading, making a small amount of invested capital work overtime. This is a dangerous disease. Its cure is more invested capital, not more debt.

Your banker and accountant can help you with this. Thinking about the right balance before you go to your financing sources will doubly protect you. Tell them what you think the proper balance is, and then ask them what kind of financing makes the most sense for you, both now and in the long run. You want to take a conservative path. It does you and your investors a favor.

Credit and debt, properly used, enable you to grow faster than an ultra-conservative no-debt strategy. To not use leverage is about as sane as playing baseball but never batting. Pure defensiveness is ultimately self-defeating.

There is a middle course between over-leverage and ultra-conservatism that's difficult to steer. It all starts by identifying legitimate business needs, testing the needs, and making rational financing decisions.

Trade and industry ratios (FRA, for example) provide a good reality check. What debt and invested capital balance does the top quartile use? Look at their Debt/Net Worth ratio and the composition of their net worth (retained earnings and invested capital). If your balance differs radically from theirs, make sure you have a good reason for your balance.

31

Where to Find Capital

Chapters 31–38 were written to help you understand a variety of sources of capital (both loans and equity).

Asset-Based Loans

These loans generally come from commercial finance companies (as opposed to banks) and are offered on a revolving basis and collateralized by a company's assets, specifically, accounts receivable and inventory.

Appropriate for: Companies that may be rapidly growing, highly leveraged, in the midst of a turnaround, or undercapitalized. In addition, asset-based financing works only for companies with proven accounts receivable and a demonstrated track record of turning over inventory several times each year.

Supply: Overall, the supply of asset-based financing is vast. A large number of commercial finance companies, as well as many banks, have massive pools of capital to lend to businesses. For asset-based loans of $500,000 or less, the market is considerably smaller. Most asset-based lenders would prefer to make larger loans because the cost to monitor an asset-based loan is generally the same whether it's large or small.

Best use: Financing rapid growth in the absence of sufficient equity capital to fund receivables and inventory. Well-suited to manufacturers, distributors, and service companies with a leveraged balance sheet whose seasonal needs and industry cycles often hamper their cash flow. Asset-based loans can also be used to finance acquisitions.

Cost: More expensive than bank financing, since asset-based lenders generally have higher expenses than bankers. Still, pricing is competitive among asset-based lenders. These loans can be pricey, though, running 12 to 28 percent.

Ease of acquisition: Comparatively easy if your company has good financial statements, good reporting systems, inventory that is not exotic, and finally, customers who have a track record of paying their bills. If you don't have any of these things, your path to an asset-based loan will be challenging.

Range of funds typically available: $250,000 to $1 million from small finance companies and financial institutions. Larger lenders tend to specialize in financing amounts of $1 million and greater.

401(k) Financing

A 401(k) is a tax-deferred savings account that an employer establishes for its employees. This savings vehicle can be used for almost any kind of investment. The 401(k) stays intact even if the employee leaves the firm. If the employee leaves to start a new business, his or her 401(k) can be used to invest in, or even to finance, the new venture.

Appropriate for: Any company at any stage of development. Since entrepreneurs fund the company with their own retirement savings, they need only convince themselves that the deal is worth the risk.

Supply: This option is for entrepreneurs who have been cut loose from corporate America with their 401(k) plans intact. Beyond the requirement of simply having a 401(k) account, the supply is further influenced by how much of their tax-deferred retirement savings entrepreneurs are willing to put at risk.

Best use: Financing startups. When startup companies are financed with equity from outside sources, it's the most expensive avenue of financing because the company is worth so little. A round of seed financing can cost 30 percent of the equity. Although 401(k) financing forces a company to surrender equity, it is surrendered to the firm's founders, which means that the ownership is not really lost.

Cost: The fees can run high because several professionals are required to engineer the transaction. However, 401(k) financing does not cost the founders any equity in their business.

Ease of acquisition: Moderately challenging. There are several legal and accounting issues that must be resolved for this technique to work properly.

Range of funds typically available: $20,000 and greater.

32

▼

Debt Management and Financing

Equipment Leasing

Equipment leasing is basically a loan in which the lender buys and owns equipment and then leases it to a business at a flat monthly rate for a specified number of months. At the end of the lease, the business may purchase the equipment for its fair market value (or for a fixed or predetermined amount), continue leasing, lease new equipment, or return it.

Appropriate for: Any business at any stage of development. For startup businesses with no revenue, "small ticket" leases, those of $100,000 or less, are generally feasible using the personal credit of the founders or owners—if they are willing to make the monthly payments.

Supply: Abundant. Of the billions of dollars individual and institutional investors pour into the capital markets each month, a good chunk finds its way to leasing companies that use these funds to purchase equipment on behalf of small businesses. With more money flowing into the markets, leasing companies are flush with capital. As a result, they are eager to do business and respond to competition with lower monthly rates.

Best use: Financing equipment purchases. Leasing can also finance the soft costs often associated with equipment purchases, such as installation and training services.

Cost: Lease financing is generally more expensive than bank financing, but in most instances, it's more easily obtained.

Ease of acquisition: Easy for leases of less than $100,000. An application for a small-ticket lease is generally no more complex than a credit card application. Leases for more than $100,000 typically require detailed financial information from the business, and the leasing company conducts a more thorough credit analysis than it would for a smaller transaction.

Range of funds available: Unlimited.

Advantages of Leasing

Equipment leasing is big business. In fact, it is the single largest source of financing for U.S. businesses, totaling more than $200 billion annually. The dollar volume of equipment leases exceeds the annual dollar volume of commercial loans. It even exceeds the dollars raised through the issuance of bonds or the sale of stock. Leasing is bigger than commercial mortgages. And, perhaps best of all, because of the high volume of available lease capital, equipment lease financing is readily obtainable for small businesses.

Here are some of the most important competitive advantages of lease financing:

▶ **100% financing:** With leasing, the lessor (that is, the company that purchases, then rents the equipment) finances 100% of the cost of the equipment being purchased. In fact, lessors often finance some of the soft costs—such as training and installation—associated with the purchase of new equipment.

▶ **Easy application and rapid approval times:** Most applications for leases of less than $75,000 (and sometimes up to $150,000) are a single page in length, and approvals can occur within 24 hours.

▶ **Favorable tax treatment:** In general, the tax implications of leasing can be complex; that topic alone could be the subject of a book. However, for small-ticket leases, which in most instances are so-called capital leases, the tax treatment is straightforward and favorable. The business leasing the equipment writes off the entire monthly payment as an expense. Conversely, when a business takes out a loan to buy equipment—which means it places it on its books as an asset—the company can only deduct the interest portion of the payment plus a depreciation expense.

▶ **Flexible terms:** Most leasing companies can structure the term of the lease to fit a certain monthly payment amount that the business owner is willing or able to make.

Companies of every size use leasing. Commercial airlines lease jets. Caterers lease tables, chairs, and chafing dishes. So how do the professionals who serve these diverse businesses segment the market? According to the Equipment Leasing Association, the leasing business is divided into three distinct markets:

1. **Small-ticket leases:** less than $250,000
2. **Middle-market leases:** $250,000 to $5 million
3. **Large-ticket leases:** greater than $5 million

▶ Credit Scoring

Credit scoring streamlines the credit process because it looks at relatively few variables out of many that constitute a company's full financial picture. Each variable is scored, and the credit decision-making is done either by computers or clerks. Often, the credit-scoring models are adjusted over time to reflect a lender's experience. As these models evolve, many lenders regard their credit-scoring system to be proprietary and a trade secret. Below are the main criteria that are evaluated in a credit-scoring system:

▶ Time in business
▶ Lessee's industry
▶ Type of equipment
▶ Bank's rating of lessee

▶ Trade creditor's rating of lessee

▶ Personal credit bureau reports on the principals

▶ Landlord rating

▶ Quality of the vendor supplying equipment to be leased

▶ Structure of the lease

▶ New or used equipment

▶ Credit reports of outside reporting agencies

Source: *The Leasing Professional's Handbook*

Community Development Financial Institutions

Community development financial institutions (CDFIs) provide loan financing to businesses in economically distressed urban and rural communities that need economic development. CDFIs make loans that are generally "unbankable" by traditional industry standards.

Appropriate for: Startup funds for established companies that can demonstrate the ability to repay a loan but whose loan proposal is unbankable because of past credit problems, the size of the loan request, limited equity from founders, or limited collateral.

Supply: Good. There are nearly 1,000 CDFIs in urban, rural, and reservation-based communities with billions of dollars to lend. Unfortunately, despite their numbers, CDFIs can be difficult to track down because they aren't as well-publicized as mainstream financing sources. The best way to find them is by networking with other entrepreneurs and local businesses.

Best use: For starting a new business or expanding an established one. Also, CDFIs are useful when the proceeds can be used to create a second bottom line in the form of community job creation through the introduction or preservation of a service that is vital to a community or stabilizing a community in decline.

Cost: Relatively inexpensive. Most CDFI loans are priced according to risk as opposed to the cost of funds. Since CDFI loans tend to be riskier than bank loans, they may cost more as well. Typical pricing may be from 0.5 to 3 percentage points higher than conventional loan rates, but in some instances, CDFI loans may be less expensive than mainstream financing. For example, a CDFI loan for a child-care facility is generally less costly than conventional credit.

Ease of acquisition: Easier than commercial lenders, but challenging, since for loans, a company must still undergo the scrutiny of a traditional credit analysis. The difficulty of securing CDFI financing is sometimes compounded by the relatively narrow focus and agenda these institutions may maintain.

Range of funds typically available: $2,000 and much higher. In fact, the National Community Capital Association reports an average member loan of $11.4 million.

33

Types of Bank Loans

Private Loan Guarantees

Private loan guarantees provide a guarantee of payment that stands behind an early-stage company and enables it to take out a loan from a bank. Conceptually, private guarantees play the same role as an SBA loan guarantee.

Appropriate for: Early-stage companies that within a year will turn the corner toward profitability or commence product sales. The limited time frame stems from the fact that loan guarantees typically only last a year, and at the end of that period, the company must be able to raise equity capital to pay off the original loan or be able to apply for and get a loan based on its own fundamentals.

Supply: Though this technique is uncommon, the supply is theoretically abundant. Specifically, any wealthy individual—for example, angel investor—willing to consider an equity investment should also be willing to consider a loan guarantee.

Best use: For companies that can put the borrowed funds to use and show an immediate result either in profitable product sales or the commercialization of a product or service concept. Loan guarantees work particularly well for very young companies that would end up selling a majority equity stake in the business if forced to use equity capital.

Cost: The fees and interest on a loan guarantee can be expensive compared with a traditional loan. However, loan guarantees make it possible for an entrepreneur to raise capital without surrendering control, which makes it cheap compared with most forms of equity financing.

Ease of acquisition: Loan guarantees are somewhat easier to negotiate than pure equity investments because the investor guaranteeing the loan never turns over any of his or her own funds, unless, of course, the company does not perform as projected.

Range of funds typically available: No upper or lower limit.

Bank Term Loans

Term loans are the basic vanilla commercial loan. They typically carry fixed interest rates and monthly or quarterly repayment schedules and include a set maturity date. Bankers tend to classify term loans into two categories, short-term (less than one year) and intermediate term (one to five years). Longer-term loans are for fixed assets such as buildings and land.

Appropriate for: Established small businesses that can leverage sound financial statements and substantial down-payments to minimize monthly payments and total loan costs. Repayment is typically linked in some way to the item financed. Term loans require collateral and a relatively rigorous approval process but can help reduce risk by minimizing costs. Before deciding to finance equipment, borrowers should be sure they can make full use of ownership-related benefits, such as depreciation, and should compare the cost with that of leasing.

Supply: Abundant but highly differentiated. The degree of financial strength required to receive loan approval can vary tremendously from bank to bank, depending on the level of risk the bank is willing to take on.

Best use: Construction; major capital improvements; large capital investments, such as machinery; working capital; purchases of existing businesses.

Cost: Inexpensive if the borrower can pass the financial litmus tests. Rates vary, making it worthwhile to shop, but they generally run around 2.5 points over prime for loans of less than seven years and 3.0 points over prime for longer loans. Fees totaling up to 1 percent are common (though this varies greatly, too), with higher fees on construction loans.

Ease of acquisition: Challenging but sometimes only a moderate challenge when smaller amounts are involved. However, for loans more than $100,000 (sometimes up to $200,000), you need a complete set of financial statements and must undergo a complete financial analysis by the lending institution.

Range of funds typically available: $25,000 and greater.

The demands of a term loan are challenging for any business. The old banking adage "they only lend money when you don't need it" is an old banking adage largely because it's true. It should not come as any surprise then that term loans are particularly difficult for small businesses.

To understand why this is so, consider two of the three primary criteria—cash flow and collateral—banks use to evaluate loan proposals. The third, incidentally, is the character of the borrower—that is, do they exhibit the kind of behavior, past and present, consistent with the repayment of debts. While the character test is easy to pass, cash flow and collateral are more daunting for small businesses.

Take the issue of collateral. Many small businesses can't collateralize a loan because they're service businesses without much in the way of tangible assets. Compounding the problem, many small business owners are cash poor; whatever assets they have are generally sunk into the business, often making their personal guarantee inadequate.

SBA Guaranteed Loans

The SBA has a wealth of programs designed to assist small businesses. Their loan guarantee program is an especially helpful resource. Go to sba.gov to find out more about their programs.

Businesses can obtain term loans from a bank or commercial lending institution of up to ten years for working capital and up to twenty-five years for real estate and equipment, with the SBA guaranteeing as much as 85 percent of the loan principal.

Appropriate for: Established small businesses capable of repaying a loan from cash flow, but whose principals may be looking for a longer term to reduce the monthly payments or may have inadequate corporate or personal assets to collateralize the loan.

Supply: Vast. The SBA guarantees some $12 billion per year in loans. That is, because of SBA loan guarantees, more than $12 billion in loans are made annually by participating lenders.

Best use: Purchasing equipment, financing the purchase of a business, and in certain instances, working capital. The SBA guarantee can help borrowers overcome the problems of a weak loan application resulting from inadequate collateral or limited operating history.

Cost: Comparatively inexpensive. Maximum allowed interest rates generally range from highs of prime plus 4.75 percentage points to prime plus 2.75 percentage points, though lenders can and often do charge less. These rates may be higher or lower than rates on nonguaranteed loans. What's more, banks making SBA loans cannot charge "commitment fees" for agreeing to make a loan, or prepayment fees on loans under fifteen years (a prepayment penalty kicks in for longer loans), which means the effective rates for SBA loans may be, in some instances, superior to those for conventional loans.

Ease of acquisition: Challenging. Although the SBA has created streamlined approaches to loan applications, conventional SBA guarantee procedures and protocols pose a significant documentation and administrative challenge for most borrowers.

Range of funds typically available: The SBA guarantees up to $1 million of loan principal.

34

What Do Bankers Look For?

Banks are custodians of their depositors' money. As such they have an overriding need to protect that money. They run on spread: they pay you little or nothing on your deposits while earning 6 percent or more on the loans they underwrite. Indeed, a bank is more accurately characterized as an intermediary than a risk taker. The bank mediates the period of time for which people want to borrow money vs. the period of time people are willing to lend it. They don't exist to lose money.

These principles speak volumes about the behavior of your commercial lender. Loans are generally fully collateralized. If not, they are personally guaranteed. Most likely, they are both. Where fixed assets are thin or nonexistent, look for accounts receivable financing to be offered in place of term loans.

If a bank lends money to a company that subsequently triples sales and quadruples earnings, the return the bank enjoys is the same as if the company had never grown a percentage point. In fact, such growth may alarm the bank, since the earnings could ultimately destabilize the company and undermine its ability to repay the loan. (For the equity investor, meteoric growth spells success, even if in the near term it leads to significant variance in earnings and cash flow.)

Bankers look first for the safety of their principal, second for returns on that principal, and third for the stability of the businesses that borrow from them. For these reasons a carefully targeted financing proposal—a specialized version of your business plan—is mandatory. While your banker may not explicitly ask for such a proposal, be proactive: the thinking you put into the proposal will go a long way toward assuaging his or her bankerly anxiety.

What is a financing proposal? At the very least, a financing proposal is a documented statement of what debt you need, why you need it, and how you plan to repay it. The documentation should include up-to-date balance sheets, cash flow pro formas, and projected P&Ls. All bankers have forms that help you prepare these but by basing your proposal on your own business plan, you up your credibility.

Your financing proposal should make clear:

▶ **How much money you want**
▶ **What you want it for**
▶ **What kind of money (debt, equity)**
▶ **When you want it**
▶ **Why it will make your business better**
▶ **How you'll pay it back**
▶ **What your contingency plans might be, just in case**

Know the kind of credit you need. The basic rule is to fit the term of the loan to the purpose. A real estate loan will run fifteen years or more, and be repaid from operating profits, while an inventory loan is short-term, and gets repaid from the inventory turnover. Some loans call for term payments that include principal and interest, others for interest only with lump sum principal reductions. The package can become complex.

If in doubt, ask your banker for advice: "I want to expand. Here's the loan I think I need. What do you think?" is a lot better than asking for the wrong loan at the wrong time in the wrong way. Your banker wants you to succeed and knows (if he or she is any good) that there's a high correlation between asking for (and heeding) professional advice and making a small business grow profitably.

Remember the six Cs of credit: character, capacity, conditions, collateral, credibility, and contingency plan. Assuming that you pass the character hurdle (no recent bankruptcies, if any, and a good track record of meeting obligations as they come due are the bare minimum here), your banker will entertain your loan proposal.

Capacity

The first thing your banker looks at is your balance sheet. If your company has a negative net worth, you won't get a loan. Next, what do your current and quick ratios say about your liquidity? What is your working capital situation? Is it up or down from last year? How do the inventories look? Are payables creeping up?

Next, your P&L gets a going over: Is your company profitable? Your banker will check your operating ratios for profitability and to see how well the business is being managed. Your coverage ratios measure your ability to take on debt. Leverage ratios measure exposure to risk and vulnerability to business downturns. The higher the leverage, the higher the risk and the higher the potential profits, but bankers are risk averse.

Conditions

This refers to the current economic climate. If times are rough (2008–2010 comes to mind) credit will be harder to obtain than in normal times. Bankers have an obligation to protect their depositors' cash, and if they think times are too risky they tend to be even more cautious than usual.

A related issue here is what the loan is for. Some banks won't lend to startups (not uncommon). Some won't lend to restaurants, or certain kinds of retail business, or to businesses that are not familiar to them. They may be loaned up in some areas—that is, have a lot of loans out to one sector.

Collateral

Bankers don't want to be second-hand dealers if you can't repay your loan, but they are interested in the quality of your collateral.

To see how the secondary source of repayment stacks up, banks typically assign the following values to assets:

▶ **Accounts receivable:** Generally speaking, lenders assign a value to the accounts receivable of about 60 percent of what a company shows on its books, but they may go as high as 75 percent on accounts less than 30 days old.

▶ **Inventory:** Figure from 0 percent to 60 percent. The greater a commodity inventory is, the more value it is assigned. If you have rolled steel and aluminum ingots, you are probably looking at the 60 percent end of the spectrum. Then again, if you have test tubes full of antigens, you might be looking at the other end.

▶ **Equipment:** Equipment is generally worth about 60 percent of the net book value, which is cost less accumulated depreciation.

Loan guarantees (private, SBA, or other) are a form of collateral that can make the difference between securing a loan or getting turned down. A cosigner lends you his or her credit rating: If the loan sours and you can't make the bank whole, your cosigner will have to pony up the necessary cash. If you do need a cosigner, make sure this is known beforehand.

Credibility

Your well-crafted financing proposal, based on your business plan, plus a record of operating profitability will give you a lot of credibility.

Contingency Plan

Create a contingency plan. A contingency plan covers the two extremes pointed out in Chapter 21, Sales and Expense Forecast. What if everything goes wrong? What fallback actions would make sense? What if sales take off like a skyrocket? Where will the resources come from to fuel that growth? The first step in contingency planning is to see what the effect will be on the P&L and cash flows. The variable expenses won't be a problem, but what about fixed expenses? Will they be covered? If not, what will be done? Bankers and other investors are invariably impressed with contingency plans, even if the contingency plans are sketchy.

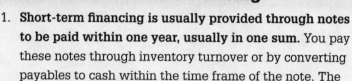

▶ Three Kinds of Bank Financing

1. **Short-term financing is usually provided through notes to be paid within one year, usually in one sum.** You pay these notes through inventory turnover or by converting payables to cash within the time frame of the note. The note may be available through a line of credit.

2. **Intermediate-term financing ranges from one to five years.** You repay these (usually) in fixed monthly payments or fixed principal payments plus interest. These loans are repaid from operating profits.

3. **Long-term financing is provided for periods longer than five years.** The most common example is real estate financing, where you pay the loan down on a prearranged schedule over a long period of years. The source of the repayment is operating profits and/or new equity.

Part Six

▼

Resources

What Other Investors Look For in a Financing Proposal

35

What Do Investors Look For?

Equity investors don't look for the characteristics that demonstrate the ability to repay a loan. They look for rapid growth. While they may write part of their investment as a loan, their primary interest is in making large gains when the company goes public, is acquired, or otherwise provides a method for them to cash out their investment. Equity investors try to understand the amount of capital a company requires as it grows. If the company requires substantially more equity capital than the investor is able or prepared to provide, perhaps it's not such a good investment.

There are two primary reasons businesses fail to raise the capital they need:

1. **The entrepreneur pursues the wrong sources of capital.**
2. **The entrepreneur fails to adequately plan for his or her search for capital.**

"Ready, fire, aim" is a common approach when it comes to raising money. But it's a recipe for disaster. Most companies have few viable investor candidates, and being ill-prepared in front of one—even though he or she is your perfect match—dramatically increases the likelihood that he or she will pass on your deal.

The following paragraphs offer a set of steps for planning and meeting with angel investors. The advice applies to any equity investor, including institutional venture capitalists, investment bankers, and reverse merger candidates.

Step 1: Revise Your Business Plan

Polish your business plan, make sure it's targeted to the prospective investor. You won't get appointments until would-be investors have looked at your business plan. Serious investors are busy people who jealously guard their time.

Here are the planning steps you should follow even before you make that first phone call to investors:

a. **Prepare a business plan.** You must have a business plan for two very good reasons. First, if your initial contact with an investor is successful, he or she will request one. When an investor asks to see a plan, or even a plan summary, it must be on his or her desk the next morning. At the very least, it must go out first-class mail that day.

   Second, investors ask a lot of questions. And it's only by writing a business plan that you can possibly hope to answer the kinds of questions an investor will ask with the kind of conviction and authority that will win the day. No entrepreneur ever has raised a single penny simply by writing a business plan. Entrepreneurs present their plan and use the thinking that went into its writing to defend their ideas, strategies, and tactics to prospective investors.

b. **Determine your sizzle.** The business plan is the steak. Now what's the sizzle? What's the one-line answer to the first question the investor will ask: "What does your business do?" The response must be brief, understandable, and memorable.

   For instance, if your business resells deep-discount travel packages for unused vacations at luxury resorts to

Fortune 1000 consumer-products companies to use as fulfillment premiums, don't say that. The investor's eyes will glaze over at the word "unused." Say: "We are a business that makes luxury travel affordable for 50 million middle-income Americans."

Then the investor will give you the opportunity to say, "Travel in the United States is a $70 billion market annually. With a market this size, there are lots of niches, and we are operating in one that has little competition and high margins."

Or, let's say your business offers physicians marketing services for elective surgical procedures that help them overcome the ceilings on fees imposed by HMOs and other third-party payers. Don't say that right off the bat. Instead, say, "We are the new breed of marketing agency that every physician now knows that she needs if she hopes to survive the changes taking place in medicine."

Such statements are your sizzle. They are succinct, memorable, and perhaps most important, repeatable. You want a sound bite an investor can easily repeat to his or her fellow investors. Even Wall Street uses this trick. When venerable motorcycle maker Harley-Davidson went public, the pitch to investors was: "Own a piece of an American icon."

c. **Form an advisory board.** Every industry has people who have succeeded. Reach out to these people, and ask for their help in the form of serving on your advisory board. There's a lot of psychology in why people readily agree to such a proposition. Many appreciate being recognized as successful. Others have a natural mentoring inclination that comes from being a successful businessperson. Some want to relive their previous success, while others would simply like to be part of a support system they wish they had had when they were starting out.

But one of the real purposes of forming an advisory board is to help generate leads. When you ask advisory board members about sources of financing, if those requests have been properly initiated, you find that many willingly share their contacts. To a lesser extent, the purpose of forming an advisory board is to increase the comfort level outside investors have with your team.

d. Focus on getting a lead investor. If you are privately raising equity capital, there's little likelihood that you'll run into one sugar daddy that will cut a check for the entire deal. It's more likely that you will run into a number of investors who will offer smaller amounts. These are helpful, but they should be found later. Initially, you must focus all your energy on finding the investor or investors who will take down 25 percent to 50 percent of your deal and who, in doing so, will provide a magnet for the smaller investors.

e. Seek legal counsel. Soliciting capital may bring several state and federal securities laws into play. You don't want to unwittingly run afoul of them, which may force you to return capital you worked so hard to raise. Even though many deals are exempt from state and federal securities laws, there can still be a host of requirements on notification, documentation, and the number of investors who can participate in the offering. Raising money is hard. Don't make it harder by unknowingly breaking the law.

f. Prepare a deal summary. Technically, this should be your business plan's executive summary. The executive summary should be no longer than two pages and must function as a stand-alone document. This summary must describe the company, product or service, market, competition, key personnel, funding required, and use of proceeds, and it must give a historical and projected financial snapshot. To stay within the necessary one- to two-page length, you should write no more than one paragraph about each item.

g. Get referrals. If an investor is interested in learning more about your business after the first telephone call or meeting, he or she might want to talk to someone else, such as a customer, licensee, franchisee, your accountant, attorney, or members of your advisory board or board of directors. Plan for this question by figuring out who should talk. That way, when an investor asks to speak with someone, you can offer a name and a phone number rather than saying "I'll get back to you on that." Remember, you may never get the investor back on the telephone again. But if he or she has an action step and takes it, the mating dance is still on track.

h. **Get introductions.** If your lead-generation process turns up investors you do not know, you must work ahead of time to get some kind of introduction. The best type is when someone calls ahead of you and warns that you'll be calling. That way, you'll get an initial telephone call with the investor nearly 100 percent of the time.

As a fallback, during the first conversation, if you can say in your first breath, "Our mutual acquaintance, Jere Calmes, suggested contacting you," chances of the call being successful—that is, the investor agreeing to look at something you send him or her—increase dramatically.

Former employees, trade associations, accountants, lawyers, or the person who supplied your lead in the first place all represent viable candidates for preparing the investor for your initial contact.

i. **Choose a meeting venue.** If you have something in your factory or office worth seeing, such as a manufacturing process, you should always try to get the investor to come to your turf for the first meeting. However, if you work in a hovel or at home, it may not be a good idea to let the investor see your space. If this is the case, plan ahead of time a variety of meeting places where you know what's going on, such as the office of your accountant or attorney or hotel lobbies you have visited that can accommodate an intimate conversation.

Step 2:   Generate Leads

You must find the kind of people who typically invest in early-stage deals. Once you learn where they are, you must qualify them.

If you trace your life's path you may see that where you have ended is to a great extent the result of chance meetings and random events. The same theory applies to raising money. You never know whom you will meet who'll put you in touch with the person who becomes your investor.

Raising money is a lot like finding a job. You must network, network, and network some more. Ask for three names from every person you meet. One entrepreneur who had diligently saved the business cards of every person he had met over the years sent each one a letter asking for help in raising money or putting him in touch with investors. He found five investors and a lot of encouragement for what he was doing.

If you're not such a pack rat, here are several paths you can take to start meeting investors:

▶ **Venture capital forums**
▶ **Fund-raising seminars**
▶ **Venture capital fairs**
▶ **Venture capital clubs**
▶ **Professionals, such as accountants and attorneys**

Step 3:   Be Responsive if There is Any Indication of Interest

Follow up, follow up, and follow up some more. Persistence pays. It's not uncommon for large venture funds to receive thousands of proposals in a year, so follow-ups are imperative.

Now it's time to dial for dollars. Before picking up the telephone, you should have created a business plan and, where possible, gained some kind of entrée to each of the investors you plan to approach. Now you must:

a. **Qualify the investor.** Your first task is to ensure you and your would-be investors are a match. This must be done early in the process. After all, every investor has parameters and preferences, and if you don't fit within them, you should probably spend your time on other potential investors.

   One of the first things the investor will ask early in your conversations is who you are and what your company does, to which you should respond with something like, "We are the business that makes luxury travel affordable for 50 million middle-income Americans."

   Next, you might suggest some overall industry trends, but then you will need to ask: "Do you typically invest in companies such as ours?" If the person you are talking to doesn't invest in companies like yours, it's time to gracefully bow out and move on. But remember to get three more names before you do.

b. **Answer questions.** If the investor has any interest, he or she will ask many questions. This is where writing a good business plan pays off. Because you've thought through every aspect of the business, you should be able to manage these questions.

It's important, however, to answer with confidence. The investor is evaluating you from the moment the conversation begins. Equity investors are unlike lenders in this regard. They don't rely on cash flow to recoup their investment. They rely instead on you, the entrepreneur, to build value and sell the business to other investors until the point where it gets sold to the public or another corporation. The upshot is, if you can't convince this investor, he or she will most likely conclude you probably can't convince the next investor, and that ultimately, his or her investment will remain trapped inside the company.

You want to show momentum because you want to leave investors with the feeling that things are happening quickly, that if they invested, their money would immediately be used productively and not sit around in limbo while you figure out the nuances of getting the business to the next stage of development.

c. **Get a meeting.** Your objective during the initial contact is to schedule a meeting with the investor. If your list of potential investors is well-qualified, meetings will come easily. If not, getting an investor to agree to a meeting will be more challenging.

If the investor is interested in meeting, he or she will request more information, usually a business plan or business plan summary. Don't agree to send it out without getting something in return. Specifically, you want the investor to agree to meet on a certain date after he or she has reviewed the plan.

Now it's up to you to make sure your business plan arrives on the investor's desk the next day. In addition, include some kind of sample or tangible evidence of your product or service. If you sell imported shelf-stable food products, this is easy. If you manufacture waterbeds, this is more difficult. Even in difficult situations, it's worth considering creative solutions. Pictures, customer testimonials, and videotapes can sometimes help bring a product or service to life. Anyone can send a bunch of papers in the mail that pile up on someone's desk. But product and service samples are picked up, toyed with—and considered.

d. **Manage objections.** Typically, seeking the first meeting presents the first wall of objections: "The product is not developed enough," "The distribution channel is too crowded," "Your management team is too thin," "It doesn't appear that you've established technical feasibility." You must anticipate these sorts of objections and be prepared to answer them calmly and gracefully.

If the investor is qualified to participate in your offering, you must be tenacious. When investors decline an opportunity, it may be because they don't understand a certain aspect of the product, market, technology, or your vision for the company. As a result, when investors say they don't want to meet, ask them why not, and then show them where their thinking is off.

e. **Prepare a formal presentation.** You can't meet with an investor without having prepared a formal presentation. Remember, the investor is evaluating your ability to sell the company because it's how he or she will eventually get a return. If you show incompetence in this arena, it spells trouble for your capital formation efforts, even if the company shows promise.

f. **Conduct the initial meeting.** The objectives for the first meeting are straightforward: First, make the investor like you. Second, commit the investor to some kind of action step.

You must get the investor to like you for a simple reason. If he or she doesn't, there's little chance the deal you are proposing will happen. Unlike a lender, who bases his or her decision on credit quality exclusively, an equity investor looks for personal chemistry, at least for early stage offerings. Without some baseline affinity for the entrepreneur and what he or she is doing, there is no basis for an investment. Also remember that an equity investor can be romanced by business ideas and people, but it's unlikely that a lender would change the lending criteria simply because he or she liked the entrepreneur.

But you must do more than simply hit it off with the person. The meeting must close with some sort of action on the part of the investor.

Finally, keep in mind that just like with the initial telephone conversation, you want to avoid ceding control of the process to the investor. Therefore, try to make the action steps conditional on a second and, ideally, closing meeting. For instance, you might say: "So you agree to try our product for two weeks and then meet with me to discuss your thoughts."

Step 4: Close The Deal

If you're lucky enough to get face time with an investor, the deal is far from closed. Stay proactive, and respond promptly to any investor requests.

If things have gone according to plan, the date for the second meeting should have been set during the first. If not, getting this second meeting might take some effort and a bit of follow-up.

Regardless, the second meeting is deal time. And even if it's not, it's certainly the time to eliminate the investors who aren't worth pursuing further.

You must pop the question in a way that involves the investor in the decision-making process. Also, you must do it in such a way that you force the investor to declare his or her interest or lack thereof. Here is a sample dialogue:

> **Entrepreneur:** *We've met twice. I appreciate the time you've taken to understand my company. Now that you know a little more, and since you clearly have some experience in these matters, I want to ask you an important question. How much capital do you think we should be raising?*
> **Investor:** *Well, I'm glad you asked that. Because I've studied your plan, and I think you'll need much more than the $500,000 you initially sought. I think you need $750,000—not right away, but shortly after you commence marketing, which, according to this plan, could happen at the end of this year.*
> **Entrepreneur:** *Comments like that let me know I've chosen the right course of action by seeking hands-on investors, who*

can provide not just capital but input. OK, of that $750,000, how much can you commit to?

Gotcha! At this point, the investor has few courses of action. He can suggest a material amount, a small amount, or no amount. If the answer is none, you can say good-bye to that investor and move on. If it's a small amount, you can solidify this investor's interest by telling him or her you're looking for a lead investor and asking if he or she will commit the dollars just suggested when a lead investor is found. Most will say yes. If the answer is a large amount, you've accomplished your objective: You've found a lead investor.

Getting from a yes to depositing money in the bank is beyond the scope of this book. However, if you have come this far in the fundraising process, you should have had at least some contact with an attorney who has significant experience in securities law. You'll now need his or her counsel in drawing up the necessary subscription documentation or in understanding the securities laws exemptions you are taking advantage of.

 MORE

▶ One, Two, Three, Go!

The 20-minute pitch is standard operating procedure. You must be able to tell your story in this amount of time. The underpinning of the presentation is your business plan. Thus, in the allotted time, you must cover the major sections of the plan. You're trying to answer the following questions in the investor's mind:

- ▶ What is the company?
- ▶ What are its strengths?
- ▶ How has it performed?
- ▶ Where is it going?
- ▶ How will it get there?
- ▶ What does it mean to me if it succeeds?

Whether you're meeting with one investor or a roomful, the best strategy is to walk them through a set of ten to fifteen slides that punctuate your remarks.

36

Lists of Investors and Their Requiements— and Costs

Business Incubators

Business incubators are a good path to capital from angel investors, state governments, economic-development coalitions, and other investors. They house several businesses under one roof or in a campus setting and offer resident companies reduced rents, shared services, and in many instances, formal or informal access to financing.

Appropriate for: Pre-revenue-stage companies to early-stage companies selling products or services.

Supply: Approximately 1,000 incubators in North America cater to high- and low-tech businesses. About 80 percent of these incubators report that they provide formal or informal access to capital.

Best use: Many types of financing may be found through incubators, which may or may not be appropriate for your business. Generally speaking, however, incubators and the kinds of investors they attract work best for companies at the earliest stages of development.

Cost: There may be many kinds of financing found through incubators, from state assistance funds based on matching private sector investments, which can be inexpensive, to straight equity investments from angel investors, which can be expensive.

Ease of acquisition: Getting into an incubator can be easy or challenging. Simply being in an incubator offers value to investors. Incubator managers know this, and as a result, many carefully screen would-be tenants to see that they match certain criteria. The good news, however, is that once you're in an incubator, the path to angels or other investors might be more direct since they tend to hover around easily identified centers of entrepreneurial activity.

Range of funds typically available: $25,000 and greater, though some incubation programs offer microloans as small as $500.

Angel Investors

Working with angel investors means acquiring venture capital from individual investors. These individuals look for companies that exhibit high-growth prospects, have a synergy with their own business, or compete in an industry in which they have succeeded.

Appropriate for: Early stage companies with no revenue or established companies with sales and earnings. Companies seeking equity capital from angel investors must welcome the outside ownership and perhaps be willing to relinquish some control. To successfully accommodate angel investors, a company must also be able to provide an "exit" to these investors in the form of an eventual public offering or buyout from a larger firm.

Supply: The supply of angel investors is large within a 150-mile radius of metropolitan areas. The more technology-driven an area's economy, the more abundant these investors are.

Best use: Runs the gamut, from companies developing a product to those with an established product or service for which they need additional funding to execute a marketing program. Also, angel investors are appropriate for companies that have increasing product or service sales and need additional capital to bridge the gap between the sale and the receipt of funds from the customer.

Cost: Expensive. Capital from angel investors is likely to cost no less than 10 percent of a company's equity and, for early stage companies, perhaps more than 50 percent. In addition, many angel investors charge a management fee in the form of a monthly retainer.

Ease of acquisition: Angels are easy to find but sometimes difficult to negotiate with because they usually do not invest in concert and may demand different terms.

Range of funds typically available: $300,000 to $5 million.

For most small or new businesses anticipating fast growth, so-called angel investors are the most appropriate source of financing. There are many reasons for this. Some of the more fundamental and important ones include:

▶ **Angel investors are one of the most abundant sources of capital in the United States.** America's 200,000 angel investors pump about $18 billion into growing businesses each year, according to Jeffrey Sohl, director of the Center for Venture Research at the University of New Hampshire. While there has been a sharp decline in investment dollars in recent years, experts consider the angel market relatively healthy, with a sustainable growth rate of new investors.

▶ **Angel investors typically provide equity capital.** For most emerging growth businesses, equity capital is appropriate because it's permanent and doesn't require monthly or quarterly interest payments.

▶ **Angel investors typically invest in business for reasons other than economics.** A desire to help young entrepreneurs and fill the role of the mentor they never had is the reason frequently cited by angels for why they invest.

▶ **The amount of capital an emerging business needs, generally from $250,000 to $5 million, matches the commitments angels typically make.**

Stalking Angels

Angel investors are at once hard to find and easy to find. The situation is analogous to searching for gold. Generally, it's difficult to track down, but once you hit a vein ... suddenly all your hard works pays off in a big way. Here are the places angels might be hiding:

▶ **Universities:** Angel investors tend to hover near university programs because of the high level of new business activity they generate. If you're looking for money, call the nearest university that has an entrepreneurship program, and make an appointment to speak with the person who runs it. Generally, such people can point you in the direction of angels.

▶ **Business incubators:** According to the National Business Incubation Association (NBIA), there are about 1,000 business incubators in North America. At first blush, incubators appear to be the mere brick-and-mortar facilities that offer entrepreneurs reasonable rents, access to shared services, exposure to professional assistance, and an atmosphere of entrepreneurial energy. But according to NBIA president and CEO Dinah Adkins, many business incubators offer formal or informal access to angel investors. Call a business incubator and ask its director if he or she can put you in touch with an angel investor. But be forewarned: The incubator may only help current tenants.

▶ **Venture capital clubs:** The tremendous wealth created through the commercialization of technology resulted in a large number of angel investors who formalized their activities into groups or clubs. These clubs actively look for deals to invest in and their members want to hear from entrepreneurs looking for capital. The 2008–2010 bust has reduced the number and level of activity of these investors, but there are signs they are coming back.

▶ **Angel confederacies:** Some angels, shunning the formality of a venture capital club, band together in informal groups that share information and deals. Members of the group often invest independently or join together to fund a company. So-called confederacies are not easy to find, but once you locate one member, you gain access to them all, a number that could top fifty investors.

Formal venture capital groups come in two stripes—those that cater to individual investors or angels, and those that target professional institutional venture capital funds. If you're pursuing angel investors, it's important to pursue the kinds of clubs that are aimed at your needs. For instance, the New York Venture Capital Group in Manhattan is a vibrant organization, but it caters mostly to professional venture capitalists. By contrast, the Western New York Venture Association in Buffalo encourages memberships for individual investors.

Dealing with Federal Securities Laws

In 1982, Congress quite accurately recognized that many of the federal securities laws on the books represented an impediment to capital formation for smaller businesses. The result was the creation of Regulation D, which, among other things, offers small companies exemptions from federal securities laws for certain kinds of transactions. There are several wrinkles to "Reg D," but there are three important rules that could influence any kind of deal you strike with an angel investor:

1. **Rule 504: This rule is the least restrictive of all the federal securities laws exemptions.** It allows issuers—that is, companies—to sell up to $1 million worth of securities during a twelve-month period with no restrictions on the number or qualifications of investors. In addition, there are no information requirements, and general solicitation and advertising of the offering are permitted. In short, by using Rule 504, a company can sell securities to anyone without providing any information and still not provoke federal securities laws.

2. **Rule 505: This rule allows companies to raise up to $5 million from thirty-five non-accredited investors and an unlimited number of accredited investors.** Reg D also defines accredited investors: There are sixteen definitions, ranging from banks and employee benefit plans to wealthy individuals. In the context of this discussion, "accredited investors" are individuals, or angels. Individuals are considered accredited if they have joint or net worth of more than $1 million or joint income in excess of $300,000. Rule 505 imposes some information-disclosure requirements on the issuer unless the securities are sold exclusively to accredited investors.

3. **Rule 506: Deals structured under Rule 506 are sometimes called "unlimited private placements" because Rule 506 can be used to raise any amount of capital.** An unlimited private placement can be sold to as many as thirty-five non-accredited investors and an unlimited number of accredited investors. Rule 506 does impose so-called sophistication

requirements on the non-accredited investors. Specifically, the company must believe that the non-accredited investors have the experience or counsel to evaluate the merits and risk of the offering.

Using rules 504, 505, and 506, small companies can escape the burden of federal securities laws. However, all states have securities laws, as well. What is exempt at the federal level may not be exempt at the state level. If your offering isn't exempt at the state level, you may find you have to file the kind of registration statement with state securities authorities that you were trying to avoid at the federal level.

As with all securities matters, it's best to check with a securities attorney before soliciting an offering or accepting money from investors

Small Business Investment Companies

Small Business Investment Companies (SBICs) and Specialized Small Business Investment Companies (SSBICs), which target entrepreneurs who have been denied the opportunity to own a business because of a social or economic disadvantage, are licensed by the SBA and have their own capital of several million dollars. They use this money, plus funds borrowed at favorable rates from an SBA-sponsored trust, to provide equity capital and long-term loans to small companies. SBICs tend to be more risk tolerant than banks or regular venture funds, specialize in a particular industry, and target young companies that aren't ready for a traditional venture deal.

Appropriate for: Companies that are capable of repaying a loan. SBICs and SSBICs participate in two SBA-sponsored programs. One of them, called the Debenture Program, provides long-term financing in the forms of loans and debt securities to companies with reliable and predictable cash flow. The SBA's Participating Securities Program, meanwhile, makes investments in early-stage companies with good sales and earnings or companies about to turn the corner toward profitability.

Supply: SBIC financing is abundant. According to the National Association of Small Business Investment Companies, there are more than 400 SBICs and SSBICs with more than $21 billion under management.

Best use: For activities that generate cash flow in a relatively short time, such as product rollout, or for additional manufacturing or service capacity for which there is a demand.

Cost: Expensive. SBICs and SSBICs charge interest, but in addition, many look for some kind of equity compensation in the companies they finance. This equity compensation is usually in the form of stock, as well as options or warrants that allow the holder to buy stock at predetermined prices for a predetermined period.

Ease of acquisition: Challenging but attainable because the company must submit itself to a traditional credit analysis to prove it can repay a loan. This hassle is countered by the fact that these investment companies are hungry for new business and can be helpful in shepherding companies through the application and due diligence process. In addition, an SSBIC or SBIC generally represents a one-stop shop, and companies need only satisfy the requirements of this single investor to obtain funding.

Range of funds typically available: $150,000 to $5 million.

Royalty Funding

Royalty financing is an advance against future product or service sales. Diverting a percentage of the product or service sales to the investor who issued the advance, pays back the advance.

Appropriate for: Established companies having a product or service or emerging companies about to launch a product with high gross and net margins. Royalty funding is best for companies with elastic pricing—that is, the ability to raise prices without impacting sales. Appropriate for companies that experience a quick cause and effect between marketing activity and sales increases.

Supply: Substantial. Royalty financing may appeal to investors who typically don't make investments in private companies. In addition, angel investors, venture capitalists, and even state, city, or regional economic development agencies can be talked into the concept of royalty financing.

Best use: Financing-intensive sales and marketing activities.

Cost: Inexpensive for companies with high-margin products or services.

Ease of acquisition: Relatively easy because the technique appeals to a wide variety of investors. In addition, because royalty financing is essentially a loan, it generally doesn't provoke state and federal securities laws.

Range of funds typically available: $50,000 to $1 million.

504 Loan Program

Established in 1986, the 504 Loan Program provides long-term, fixed-rate financing for major fixed assets, such as real estate, facilities construction or expansion, or other fixed-asset needs. Certified Development Companies (CDCs) make 504 loans.

Appropriate for: Businesses that fall into SBA-sized ranges and whose owners are interested in reducing the costs of real estate and equipment loans.

Supply: Availability of funds is not a problem. In fiscal year 2006 (the most recent total available as of this writing), the 504 program produced 1,780 loans amounting to more than $1.33 billion for an average loan of $553,000. However, access to funds is limited by CDC locations, since these loans are meant to fund businesses within their community or region. Thus, if there is no CDC in your area, availability of these funds may present a problem.

Best use: Proceeds from these loans may be used for a variety of fixed-asset projects, such as purchasing land, making improvements, including fixing up existing buildings; grading; making street improvements; upgrading utilities; adding parking lots and landscaping; building new facilities or modernizing, renovating, or converting existing facilities; or purchasing long-term machinery and equipment.

Cost: Interest rates on 504 loans are tied to an increment above the current market rate for 5- and 10-year U.S. Treasury issues. Fees total approximately 3 percent of the loan amount and may be financed by the loan. Generally, project assets are used as collateral, and personal guarantees from the principal owners are required.

Ease of acquisition: 504 loans can be challenging. Federal regulation combined with several parties involved in the transaction make for a complex application process.

Range of funds typically available: $1 million for up to 10 years on equipment and 20 years for real estate. The maximum loan amount may be increased to $1.3 million under certain circumstances. The private lender contribution is unlimited.

The 504 Loan Program provides low-cost, fixed-rate, long-term financing to small businesses that cannot obtain funds from conventional sources. Lower down payments than traditional lenders require, usually 20 to 25 percent, and below-market rates allow small businesses to conserve working capital, and longer terms reduce monthly debt payments.

On the other hand, startups without adequate capitalization may find it difficult to obtain a 504 loan due to significant equity, or down payment requirements. Making it more difficult, if the borrower has been in operation for two years or less, the equity requirement increases from the 10 percent for more mature companies to 15 percent.

Companies considering refinancing or moving after a few years might not want to apply for a 504 loan due to prepayment penalties attached to the CDC portion of the financing for the first half of the term of the loan. Finally, because of employment requirements, these loans are not for companies looking to reduce their staff through the acquisition of high-tech equipment, etc.

37

Institutional
Venture Investors

L ess than 0.01 percent of startups receive venture capital, and that number is going down fast as the venture capital industry continues to flounder. The hockey stick projections needed to meet venture capitalists' hurdle rates are just plain ridiculous for almost all small businesses, yet many books and articles have been written about how to get money out of these notoriously beady-eyed organizations. Don't waste your time. Small businesses start with mattress or house money (personal assets or home equity) and use a great deal of bank and trade credit. Venture capitalists don't play in this game.

If your company is growing explosively, with consistent 35 to 50 percent internal rates of return, a proprietary technology, or market dominance, and a need for $1 million in new investment or more, you qualify for the attention of an institutional venture capital firm. You also qualify for the interest of boutique investment banks that specialize in your kind of business. If you're in a high-growth industry and have the above qualifications, investors eager to make your acquaintance will besiege you.

In 2009, venture capital firms invested about $21 billion in 1,774 deals, for an average of $1.2 million per deal. The hot markets were healthcare (33 percent of total funding) and Internet companies (27 percent). Technology-oriented companies (Internet, mobile and telecom, software and computer hardware) accounted for 50 percent of total funding.

Venture Capital Firms

This type of funding includes venture capital from professionally managed funds that have between $25 million and $1 billion to invest in emerging growth companies.

Appropriate for: High-growth companies capable of reaching at least $25 million in sales in five years.

Supply: Limited. According to recent surveys from the National Venture Capital Association, U.S. venture capital firms annually invest between $5 billion and $10 billion. Many of these investment dollars go to companies already in the institutional venture capitalist's portfolio.

Best use: Varied. May be used for everything from financing product development to expansion of a proven and profitable product or service.

Cost: Expensive. Institutional venture capitalists demand significant equity in a business. The earlier the investment stage, the more equity is required to convince an institutional venture capitalist to invest.

Ease of acquisition: Difficult. Institutional venture capitalists are choosy. Compounding the degree of difficulty is the fact that institutional venture capital is an appropriate source of funding for a limited number of companies.

Range of funds typically available: $1 million and up.

38

IPOs, Reverse Mergers, and Other Exotica

Initial Public Offering

An *initial public offering* (IPO) is the sale of equity in a company, generally in the form of shares of common stock, through an investment banking firm. These shares subsequently trade on a recognized stock market. For small emerging companies, the stock market will probably be the NASDAQ SmallCap market or the NASDAQ National Market System.

Appropriate for: Startup to established companies. Startup companies must demonstrate the potential to develop into profitable enterprises that will deliver significant annual increases in sales and earnings. Established companies must also demonstrate significant future growth potential. In either case, minimum earnings growth potential is 20 percent per year, and the company should be able to achieve a valuation (total shares outstanding times their price) of at least $100 million to be truly successful as a publicly held corporation.

Supply: Theoretically abundant. In the United States, investors pour billions of dollars into the equity markets each month, and several billion dollars find their way into smaller IPOs. However, for conventional IPOs, the true supply is much smaller and is ultimately governed by the number of investment banking firms and their willingness to underwrite the offering.

Best use: Financing the expansion of manufacturing or service capacity or marketing activities having immediate impact on earnings. Also, providing a company with increasing sales, as a layer of working capital to fund growing inventory (if there is any) or accounts receivable. IPO funds can be used to finance research and development, but stock prices tend to decline during prolonged periods of product development, which in turn generates new challenges for founders or senior management.

Cost: IPOs are perhaps the most expensive way to finance a company. Not only will an IPO cost a significant chunk of the company's equity—no less than 25 percent and perhaps a great deal more—but fees and expenses can climb to as much as 25 percent of the deal. For a $5 million offering, that's $1.25 million.

Ease of acquisition: Unreasonably difficult. Going public is one of the most challenging transactions. During robust economic periods, about 750 to 1,000 companies go public each year in offerings underwritten by investment banking firms. Many more try but fail during the process. For the first seven months of 2009, 13 companies went public and raised a total of $4.25 billion.

Range of funds typically available: $5 million and greater.

Direct Public Offering

Direct public offerings (DPOs) are the direct sale of shares in a company to individual investors. After the shares are sold, investors may or may not trade on a stock market or exchange.

Appropriate for: Established companies, but DPOs can also be used for startup and emerging companies. One of the most important characteristics a company should possess for a successful DPO is a strong affinity for its customers, the surrounding community, or the industry in which it does business. In a DPO, these affinity groups become the company's shareholders.

Supply: Vast. For years, individual investors have heard about the millions, and in some cases billions, of dollars being made by venture capitalists through investments in companies in their formative stages of development. These same investors would like the chance to play venture capitalist, and your DPO may give them that opportunity.

Best use: Financing the expansion of profitable operations. DPOs can be used to finance research and development but public investors become impatient during long periods of product development. When they are unhappy, they can cause problems for the company later as it tries to raise money to finance the marketing and the rollout of the product or service.

Cost: Expensive. A DPO is less expensive than an IPO with an investment banker, but only moderately so. The absence of an underwriter's commission is sometimes more than offset by the marketing expenses a company must bear in a DPO. In addition, like a conventional IPO, the company must surrender a significant portion of ownership to its DPO investors.

Ease of acquisition: Difficult. Any transaction that involves securities is challenging. The absence of an underwriter can make the process at once easier and harder. It can make the process easier because the company can call the shots without recrimination. It can make things harder because an underwriter has experience with IPOs, and a company typically does not.

Range of funds typically available: $500,000 and greater.

Reverse Merger

A privately held company acquires a publicly traded, but usually dormant company. By doing so, the private company becomes public.

Appropriate for: Reverse mergers are appropriate for companies that don't need capital quickly and that will experience enough growth to reach a size and scale at which they can succeed as a public entity. Minimum sales and earnings to reach this plateau are $20 million in annual sales and $2 million in net earnings.

Supply: There are thousands of dormant public companies, sometimes called shells, that might be viable merger candidates. By becoming public, a company becomes a more attractive investment opportunity to a wider range of investors. The supply of equity capital is more abundant for public companies than for private ones.

Best use: Reverse mergers can be used to finance anything from product development to working capital needs. However, they work best for companies that don't need capital quickly. Not that jreverse mergers take long to consummate, but the initial transaction is usually just the halfway point. Once public, a company generally must still find capital. Also, this financing technique works better for companies that will experience substantial enough growth to develop into a real public company.

Cost: Expensive. Compared with a conventional initial public offering (IPO), however, fees and expenses are not that high for a reverse merger. Deals can be completed for $100,000, which might be 25 percent of the out-of-pocket costs that come with a full-blown IPO, but fees can reach $400,000. In the process of making the deal, however, the acquiring company might give up 10 to 20 percent of its equity. It means a company is surrendering ownership just for the privilege of being public. More equity will probably disappear when the company actually raises money.

Ease of acquisition: Difficult but not as difficult as a conventional IPO. Perhaps the most challenging aspect of a reverse merger is trying to create a real trading market for the company's shares once the deal is done.

Range of funds typically available: $500,000 and greater.

39

Conclusion

You have a limited number of strategies to adopt when you take on the management of a small and growing business. You can trust its future to luck. You can hope that your current policies will continue to work in the future. Both of these may work in the short term but almost certainly will fail in the long run. Change is the only constant.

The best strategy you can adopt is careful and intentional use of information. You need information about what is going on in your world. What is the economy doing? How is your market niche holding up as the economy changes, the market itself changes, and competitors both direct and indirect are emerging? How are technologies going to affect your business? Much of this information is informal, non-quantified or only incidentally quantified. For example, growth or decline in the Gross Domestic Product can be expressed as "up 3.2% for the previous quarter, up 2.9% for the previous year" or "economic conditions are improving." To take this as good or bad for your business depends on your knowledge of other factors: your local economy, your products and services, your customers, your ability to take advantage of change.

Your basic financial statements look backwards: your balance sheet, profit and loss statement and statement of cash flows cover determinate dates: specific days for balance sheets, the past month or quarter or year for profit and loss statements, similar periods for the statement of cash flows. Your financials are a rich source of information on how well your non-financial strategies and policies are working and how they might be improved. As a wise business owner you want to take advantage of this information.

Now look forward. Your most recent financial statements provide a base for forecasts. The most important forecasts by far are the cash budget, a budget based on projecting sales and expenses as dollars flow in and out, and the profit and loss based budget that presents an accrual approach. You must be aware of the contexts these projections anticipate.

Business does not operate in a vacuum. The book industry, for example, is looking at dramatic changes. More and more books are available in digital form. The traditionally heavy investment in PP&I (printing paper and ink) is going to be sharply reduced in the future. Returns, a traditional bugaboo of the industry, will drop precipitately as major bookstores and the big discounters turn more and more to digital delivery of books. Amazon is already doing this. Due to these profound shifts in the book business model, extrapolating traditional financial statements simply will not work. Hint: No business is immune to technological changes.

The need for financial projections, though, won't go away. You will still have to set budgets that help you to control your business, make a reasonable profit and remain solvent. Sales projections, based on the many environments your business is affected by, still must be made. Expenses still have to be forecast — the shape of those expenses will change (look at the publishing industry!) but the same basic categories will still be used.

Deviation analysis spotlights areas where performance and budget differ on a monthly and year-to-date basis. This is an invaluable aid to using a budget to control expenses. The cash flow projection or cash budget, corrected periodically for changes, will continue to be the small business owner's best insurance and control. Of course a budget is only as strong as the assumptions it is based on, hence the need for caution, completeness and awareness when setting the budget.

Analytic tools (ratio analysis prominent among them) will continue to help bankers and other investors (including you) make decisions.

Up to this point the emphasis is on controlling your business, using the financials as indispensable tools. A well-managed (e.g. controlled) business will attract financing in any economy, up or down. The emphasis in *Financing and Controlling Your Small Business* is on understanding and using financial statements and unpacking the information they contain. Obtaining financing may be one of the benefits you gain from this understanding but it pales in comparison to the benefits a tightly run business brings you.

Take care of your business, the saying goes, and it will take care of you. In the long run the value you can build into your business will provide big returns when it comes time to sell or otherwise dispose of your business. Think long-term. Use your financial statements to control and grow your business. You will be glad you did.

Glossary

Accounting: The practice of systematically recording, presenting, and interpreting the financial activities of the business.

Accounts payable: A company liability that represents amounts due for goods or services purchased on credit.

Accounts receivable: A company asset that represents amounts owed for goods and services sold on credit.

Accrual accounting: A method of accounting that records transactions as they occur, whether or not cash changes hands. Contrast with cash accounting.

Acid test ratio: Cash, plus other assets that can be immediately converted to cash, should equal or exceed current liabilities. The formula used to determine the ratio is as follows: Cash + Receivables (net) + Marketable Securities – Current Liabilities The acid test ratio is one of the most important credit barometers used by lending institutions, as it indicates the ability of a business enterprise to meet its current obligations.

Aging receivables: A listing of accounts receivable according to the length of time they have been outstanding. This shows which accounts are not being paid in a timely manner and may reveal any difficulty in collecting long overdue receivables. This may also be an important indicator of developing cash flow problems.

Amortization: To liquidate on an installment basis; the process of gradually paying off a liability over a period of time; e.g., a mortgage is amortized by periodically paying off part of the face amount of the mortgage.

Angel investor: A private individual who invests money in a business

Assets: The valuable resources or properties and property rights owned by an individual or business enterprise.

Audited financial statements: Financial statements that offer the highest level of assurance by outside independent accountants that they constitute a fair representation of the company's financial position and operating results.

Balance sheet: An itemized statement that lists the total assets, liabilities, and net worth of a given business to reflect its financial condition at a given moment in time.

Bookkeeping: The only word in the English language with three sets of double letters.

Break-even analysis: A method of analyzing the relation of fixed and variable expenses to determine at what sales level the business neither makes nor loses money.

Capital: Those funds that are needed for the base of the business. Usually they are put into the business in a fairly permanent form such as in fixed assets or plant and equipment, or are used in other ways that are not recoverable in the short run unless the entire business is sold.

Capital equipment: Equipment used to manufacture a product, provide a service, or to sell, store, and deliver merchandise. Such equipment will not be sold in the normal course of business but will be used and worn out or be consumed over time as business is conducted.

Cash accounting: A method of accounting in which only cash transactions are recorded. Contrast with accrual accounting. (You need both forms to properly manage your business.)

Cash flow: The actual movement of cash within a business: cash inflow – cash outflow. A term used to designate the reported net income of a corporation plus amounts charged off for depreciation, depletion, amortization, and extraordinary charges to reserves, which are bookkeeping deductions and not actually paid out in cash. Used to offer a better indication of the ability of a firm to meet its own obligations and to pay dividends, rather than the conventional net income figure.

Cash position: See Liquidity.

Collateral: An asset pledged to a lender to support the loan.

Chart of accounts: The heart of your accounting and bookkeeping systems. A list of the individual line items in your financial statements.

Collateral: Anything of value that can be pledged against a loan, including stocks and bonds, equipment, home equity, inventory, and receivables. If you can't repay the loan, the lender will look to your collateral as a backup source of repayment.

Common stock: Shares of stock that make up the total ownership of a company.

Common size financial statements: Financial statements expressed as percent of sales (for income statements) or percent of total assets (for the balance sheet). This permits comparing businesses of different sizes.

Comparative financial statements: A way to compare financial statements between businesses, or between different time periods for the same business. Used to spot trends and highlight areas of concern.

Cost of goods sold: The cost that a business incurs to produce a product for sale to its customers.

Cost of Sales (COS): Expenses directly incurred in sales, including but not limited to sales commissions, delivery expenses, and (most important) various inventory costs.

Current assets: Cash or other items that will normally be turned into cash within one year, and assets that will be used up in the operations of a firm within one year.

Current liabilities: Amounts owed that will ordinarily be paid by a firm within one year. Such items include accounts payable, wages payable, taxes payable, the current portion of a long-term debt, and interest and dividends payable.

Current ratio: A ratio of a firm's current assets to its current liabilities. Because a current ratio includes the value of inventories that have not yet been sold, it does not offer the best evaluation of the firm's current status. The acid test ratio, covering the most liquid of current assets, produces a better evaluation.

Debt: Debt refers to borrowed funds, whether from your own coffers or from other individuals, banks or institutions. It's generally secured with a note, which in turn may be secured by a lien against property or other assets. Ordinarily, the note states repayment and interest provisions, which vary greatly in both amount and duration, depending on the purpose, source, and terms of the loan. Some debt is convertible; i.e., it may be changed into direct ownership of a portion of a business under certain stated conditions.

Debt financing: Capital in the form of a loan, which must be repaid.

Depreciate: The ability to write off each year the cost of equipment, vehicles, or other fixed assets.

Depreciation: Allocation of the cost resulting from the purchase of a fixed asset over the entire period of its use.

Deviation analysis: The comparison of actual performance against budgeted performance, on either a monthly or year-to-date basis. Used to make sure that the business is on track toward achieving the owners' goals.

Dividend: The portion of a corporation's earnings that is paid to its stockholders.

Due diligence: An investor's investigation of a proposed deal and of the principals offering it before the transaction is finalized; generally performed by the investor's attorney and accountant.

Efficiency ratios: Ratios that measure the efficiency of the business, especially as it handles its inventory and receivables.

Equity: The owners' investment in the business. Unlike capital, equity is what remains after the liabilities of the company are subtracted from the assets—thus it may be greater than or less than the capital invested in the business. Equity investment carries with it a share of ownership and usually a share in profits, as well as some say in how the business is managed.

Equity financing: Capital received in exchange for part ownership of a company.

Extraordinary gains: Earnings from irregular occurrences such as insurance settlements or sale of assets like a company truck.

Extraordinary losses: Losses from irregular occurrences such as insurance settlements or sale of assets like a company truck; often a one-time occurrence.

Factoring: The selling of a business's accounts receivables to a factor, who immediately pays the amount of the receivables, less a discount, and receives the payments when they arrive from customers.

Filing date: The date on which a registration statement is received by the SEC.

Financial statements: Highly formatted statements used to measure the financial performance of the business. These statements compile the information gathered in the general ledger in a summary form.

Fixed expenses: Normal operating expenses of the business that are incurred whether or not sales are made; e.g., salaries, rent, interest payments.

Fiscal year: A 12-month period ending on the last day of a month other than December.

First-round financing: Money needed to actually get a company into business—that is, to start sales; follows seed funding, which is used to get a company organized and up to the verge of entering the market.

General and administrative expenses: Periodic expenses incurred in running a business as opposed to those that can be directly allocated to the cost of producing a product or providing a service.

General ledger: The summary ledger that contains all the information needed to generate the financial statements.

Gross margin: Gross profit divided by sales.

Gross profit (or gross profit margin): Net sales (sales – returned merchandise, discounts, or other allowances) minus the cost of goods sold.

Income: Money received for goods or services produced or as a return on investment.

Income statement: A statement of income and expenses for a given period.

Initial public offering (IPO): The first sale of securities (almost always stock) in a corporation under the regulations governing a public company.

Inventory: Materials owned and held by a business firm, including new materials, intermediate products and parts, work-in-process, and finished goods, intended either for internal consumption or for sale.

Journals: The books of original entry in an accounting and bookkeeping system. Journals contain the daily transactions of the business, which are then gathered into ledgers. *See Ledgers.*

Ledgers: Summarize the journal items, and in turn is summarized in the general ledger. A group of accounts.

Leverage: Ratio of debt to equity; "highly leveraged" refers to a company with a high ratio of debt to equity; borrowed funds are generally used to increase a business' buying power.

Leveraged buyout: The acquisition of a company with a high portion of borrowed funds.

Liabilities: The obligations for which a company has to pay money to others as shown on its balance sheet.

Line of credit: An agreement between a lender and a customer whereby the bank agrees to lend the customer funds up to an agreed maximum amount; generally used for seasonal needs to finance inventory and/or accounts receivable.

Liquidity: A term used to describe the solvency of a business, and which has special reference to the degree of readiness in which assets can be converted into cash without a loss. Also called cash position. If a firm's current assets cannot be converted into cash to meet current liabilities, the firm is said to be illiquid.

Loan agreement: A document that states what a business can or can't do as long as it owes money to (usu-

ally) a bank. A loan agreement may place restrictions on the owners' salaries, or dividends, on amount of other debt, on working capital limits, on sales, or on the number of additional personnel.

Loans: Debt money for private business is usually in the form of bank loans, which, in a sense, are personal because a private business can be harder to evaluate in terms of creditworthiness and degree of risk. A secured loan is a loan backed up by a claim against some asset(s) of a business. An unsecured loan is backed by the faith the bank has in the borrowers' ability to pay back the money.

Long-term liabilities: Liabilities (expenses) that will not mature within the next year.

Mezzanine financing: The final round of nonpublic financing in a rapidly growing company; allows a company to expand its operations sufficiently to qualify for an initial public offering.

Mixed expenses: Expenses that are part fixed, part variable.

Multiple-step format: A modification of the basic income statement, in which sales, cost of sales, and gross profit (or gross margin) are broken out. This contrasts with the single-step format, in which operating and other expenses are deducted directly from gross sales.

NASDAQ National Market System: the upper tier of the over-the-counter stock market where large companies trade

NASDAQ SmallCap Market: The second tier of the NASDAQ for those companies that don't meet the requirements of the NASDAQ National Market System.

Net discretionary income: Income available to pay cash dividends, repurchase common stock, retire debt, etc., after funding all investment projects.

Net margin: The ratio of net income to net sales.

Net worth: The owners' equity in a given business represented by the excess of the total assets over the total amounts owed to outside creditors (total liabilities) at a given moment in time. Also, the net worth of an individual as determined by deducting the amount of all his or her personal liabilities from the total value of his personal assets. Generally refers to tangible net worth; i.e., does not include goodwill, etc.

Net worth: Also called book value. Total assets − total liabilities = net worth (by definition).

Ownership structure: The legal structure of the business e.g., sole proprietorship, partnership, or corporation.

Noncash expense: A cost, such as a depreciation, depletion, or amortization, that doesn't involve cash flow but is shown on the income statement.

Note: The basic business loan, a note represents a loan that will be repaid, or substantially reduced 30, 60, or 90 days later at a stated interest rate. These are short term, and unless they're made under a line of credit, a separate loan application is needed for each loan and each renewal.

Notes payable: Short-term notes of less than one year, either under

lines of credit or with a stated repayment date.

Offering memorandum: A description of a securities offering, which is required to disclose all the factors a prospective investor would need to make a rational decision.

Operating expenses: The selling, general, and administrative expenses incurred by a business

Operating income: Gross profit − general and administrative expenses.

Operating margin: The ratio of operating margin to net sales.

Owners' equity: Excess of total assets minus total liabilities.

Partnership: A legal relationship created by the voluntary association of two or more persons to carry on as co-owners of a business for profit; a type of business organization in which two or more persons agree on the amount of their contributions (capital and effort) and on the distribution of profits, if any.

Primary research: Original research conducted by an individual or organization.

Private placement: The private sale of securities to raise capital.

Pro forma: A projection or an estimate of what may result in the future from actions in the present. A pro forma financial statement is one that shows how the actual operations of a business will turn out if certain assumptions are realized.

Profit: The excess of the selling price over all costs and expenses incurred in making a sale. Also, the reward to the entrepreneurs for the risks assumed by them in the establishment, operations, and management of a given enterprise or undertaking.

Profit & Loss (P&L): A common name for the Income Statement.

Profitability ratios: Ratios that measure the profitability of the business as a percentage of gross revenues (or sales).

Promissory note: A document that details the principal and interest owed on a loan and when payments are due; also outlines the events that would allow the bank to declare the loan in default.

Public company: A corporation allowed to sell securities to large numbers of people without having to investigate or qualify its investors.

Public shell: A publicly traded company that's dormant.

Ratio analysis: An analytic technique that relates elements of the balance sheet, profit & loss, and cash flows. The ratios express the relationships in and between these financial statements, presenting the business owner with a wealth of management information.

Regulation A filings: Securities filings that exempt small public offerings (less than $5 million) from most registration requirements with the SEC.

Regulation D: The basic federal law governing private offerings of securities.

Revenue recognition policies: The point in time during the sales cycle that a company reports its revenue on its books.

Sales: The gross amount of revenue generated by a business.

SB-1: A form used by small businesses to register offerings of up to $10 million worth of securities, provided the company has not registered more than $10 million in securities offerings during the preceding 12 months.

SB-2: A form used by small businesses to register securities to be sold to the public.

SCOR offering: Small Company Offering Registration permits a company to raise up to $1 million in a 12-month period without registering with the SEC.

Secondary research: Research that has been published and may be found in the public domain.

Second-round financing: The money raised and used for the expansion of a company that has demonstrated a basic viability in the market.

Securities: A company's stocks, bonds, promissory notes, and other financial obligations.

Seed money: The earliest investment in a company; usually in place before it's even organized as a company; commonly used to investigate a market or develop product technology.

Small Business Investment Companies (SBICs): Privately owned venture capital firms, licensed by the SBA, that invest their own capital along with money they've borrowed at a favorable rate from the government; SBICs may offer management services in addition to funding.

Solvency ratios: Ratios used to measure the liquidity of the business.

Sole proprietorship or proprietorship: A type of business organization in which one individual owns the business. Legally, the owner is the business and personal assets are typically exposed to liabilities of the business.

Specialized Small Business Investment Companies (SSBICs): Privately owned venture capital firms that serve socially and economically disadvantaged entrepreneurs by investing in companies in economically depressed areas and those owned by women, minorities, and armed services veterans.

Statement of cash flows: The financial statement that identifies the movement of cash into and out of the business during the pertinent period.

Sub-chapter S corporation or tax option corporation: A corporation that has elected under sub-chapter S of the IRS Tax Code (by unanimous consent of its shareholders) not to pay any corporate tax on its income and, instead, to have the shareholders pay taxes on it, even though it's not distributed. Shareholders of a tax option corporation are also entitled to deduct, on the individual returns, their shares of any net operating loss sustained by the corporation, subject to limitations in the tax code. In many respects, sub-chapter S permits a corporation to behave for tax purposes as a proprietorship or partnership.

Takeover: The acquisition of one company by another company.

Subordinated: In reference to debt, a loan that's paid off after other debts have been repaid.

Tax loss carryforward: A loss that can be carried forward in time to offset taxable income in a given year.

Term loans: Either secured or unsecured, usually for periods of more than a year to as many as 10 years. Term loans are paid off like a mortgage: so many dollars per month for so many years. The most common uses of term loans are for equipment and other fixed asset purposes, for working capital, and for real estate.

Trial balance: The final step in the bookkeeping process, in which debits and credits for the pertinent period are forced into balance. The trial balance ensures that the financial statements drawn from the general ledger will be accurate.

Underwriter: Investment banker or broker who agrees to purchase and resell securities to the public.

Variable expenses: Expenses that rise or fall with the level of sales.

Venture capitalists: Institutional venture capital firms that invest other people's money and manage it for them; typically seek a high degree of involvement and expect a high rate of return in a short amount of time.

Working capital: The difference between current assets and current liabilities. Contrasted with capital, a permanent use of funds, working capital cycles through your business in a variety of forms: inventories, accounts and notes receivable, and cash and securities.

Index